Le Grand Voyage

"The theological virtues of faith, hope, and charity apply not only to our relationship with God, but to our lives with one another. Seitz movingly depicts how this is so in this tender account of his time with his wife Elizabeth in France during the last years of her life. Imbued with gentle humor, sympathetic if sometimes wry social observation, and the deep current of love, this book is a testimony in miniature to the vivifying and sanctifying power of human affection in the eyes of God."

—**Ephraim Radner**, Professor Emeritus of Historical Theology, Wycliffe College, University of Toronto

"Chris Seitz's *Le Grand Voyage* is a travelogue of a trip none of us would choose, yet every one of us must, in some way, venture. Seitz gives us a beautifully told memoir of a life richly shared together, an unsentimental account of suffering and death's unwelcome intrusion, and a moving witness to love's tenacity in the face of loss. This is a love story—honest, tender, and theologically wise—in which grief is not love's defeat but its continuation. 'Unspent love.' In these pages, sorrow is not denied, death is not romanticized, and yet love, by grace, refuses to yield. Heartbreaking and hopeful, this book is a testimony to the resilience of human love and to the mercy of God who sustains even in the valley of loss."

—**Will Willimon**, Professor of the Practice of Christian Ministry, Duke Divinity School

"Chris Seitz tells a moving, profound, and cultured story of adventure, loss, and love. It is presented not in an obvious linear fashion but in a manner of re-presentation, often looping back as the priceless past interrupts the storytelling, painting vignettes in such a way that fact and meaning are mixed together. The prose is often raw, but never rough. It breathes words of life drawn from scripture and precious experience."

—**Mark Elliott**, Honorary Professor, School of Divinity, University of St Andrews

"At once candid and consoling; memories of a particular love and loss which will bring tears of recognition to others who have loved and grieved. Chris Seitz's honesty and ability to describe so exquisitely the joy of life with Elizabeth—and then its loss—is a testament to the truth that grief is indeed unspent love, and that great love has no conclusion. Seitz describes his particular experience while at the same time drawing us deeper into the Love who every grief has known."

—**L. Ann Jervis**, Professor Emerita of New Testament, Wycliffe College, University of Toronto

"*Le Grand Voyage* recounts a storybook life in France, an unimaginable victory over a fatal disease, followed by a tragic turn—death comes for the victor(s) all the same. Part memoir, part theologically informed meditation on grief, the author interrogates disorienting loss in the light of eternity. Others will find here echoes of the particularities of their own losses and recognize those precious intuitions of one's beloved in the eternal present of God."

—**Claire Mathews McGinnis**, Professor, Theology Department, Loyola University Maryland

"Many of us have benefited from Dr Seitz's scholarly work, combining as he does profound learning and passionate love for Christ and his church. In this book we benefit from something different: his deep love for his late wife. It is a beautiful, tragic story, an elegy to the great love of his life, now departed, an example of deep mourning, though, as St. Paul would remind us, mourning that is not without hope. It is this generation's *A Grief Observed*, painfully honest and touchingly human—a book from which all of us can learn."

—**Carl R. Trueman**, Professor of Biblical and Theological Studies, Grove City College

Le Grand Voyage

Life, Loss, Love

CHRISTOPHER SEITZ

CASCADE *Books* • Eugene, Oregon

LE GRAND VOYAGE
Life, Loss, Love

Copyright © 2026 Christopher R. Seitz. All rights reserved. Except for brief quotations in critical publications or reviews, no part of this book may be reproduced in any manner without prior written permission from the publisher. Write: Permissions, Wipf and Stock Publishers, 199 W. 8th Ave., Suite 3, Eugene, OR 97401.

Cascade Books
An Imprint of Wipf and Stock Publishers
199 W. 8th Ave., Suite 3
Eugene, OR 97401

www.wipfandstock.com

PAPERBACK ISBN: 978-1-6667-1159-2
HARDCOVER ISBN: 978-1-6667-1160-8
EBOOK ISBN: 978-1-6667-1161-5

Cataloguing-in-Publication data:

Names: Seitz, Christopher R. [author].

Title: Le grand voyage : life, loss, love / by Christopher Seitz.

Description: Eugene, OR: Cascade Books, 2026

Identifiers: ISBN 978-1-6667-1159-2 (paperback) | ISBN 978-1-6667-1160-8 (hardcover) | ISBN 978-1-6667-1161-5 (ebook)

Subjects: LCSH: Autobiography. | Love. | Americans—France. | Terminally ill. | Bereavement—Religious aspects—Christianity. | Consolation. | Death—Religious aspects—Christianity. | Île-de-France (France).

Classification: BV4905.2 S45 2026 (paperback) | BV4905.2 (ebook)

VERSION NUMBER 04/27/26

"For Grief" from *TO BLESS THE SPACE BETWEEN US: A BOOK OF BLESSINGS* by John O'Donohue, copyright © 2008 by John O'Donohue. Used by permission of Doubleday, an imprint of the Knopf Doubleday Publishing Group, a division of Penguin Random House LLC. All rights reserved.

Quand on n'a que l'amour
À s'offrir en partage
Au jour du grand voyage
Qu'est notre grand amour

Contents

Acknowledgments

MANY PEOPLE HAVE HELPED bring this project into book form. I am grateful to Robin Parry and the fine staff at Cascade Books. I needed Robin's counsel at several points along the way as this was a personal book and I am close to it in a different way than other books I have written.

Friends where I live in the United States generously read portions of the material. I was trying to organize three different angles of vision from three sections written at different times and bring them into a single frame and a single telling. Laura Schuler, Karen Kutsko, and Sheila Butler read and offered encouragement. The parish church alongside the Broad River, where my wife and I worshiped, has become a family where I have served since Elizabeth's death. Thank you, Rev'd Claudia Carucci, for counsel at one difficult phase of this journey.

I am grateful to James Tootle who carefully serialized the episodes of Part One for the website of French Affaires, the business I inherited and have managed after the death of my wife. I could not bear to say goodbye to her beloved investment in France and in making the French way of life come alive for so many guests over the years. Thanks to all those who read the web installments as they arrived week by week and who offered their responses. I have a slightly different ending to Part One at www.frenchaffaires.com due to only sharing that part of the present book for that context.

This book could not have been written without the love and support of so many friends of Elizabeth and me, in France and in the United States, during her journey with LAM disease and then when I lost her on September 23, 2021.

Thank you to my family, Anna, Tom, Mark, Kathleen and Peter Seitz.

In France, where Elizabeth and I shared a life with villagers and close friends: thank you, Nicole, Martine, Eric, Jean, Brigitte, Jean, Patrick,

Isabelle, Gilles, Maria and Adelino, Eric and Claire Sander. Thank you, Maud Hacker, my precious friend and colleague at French Affaires. Your companionship and excellent work have kept French Affaires and me both alive. We have ventured down many fun and rich roads together.

A special debt of gratitude goes to my neighbor Cindy Heath. You sat with me in my grief, in my pain, and offered nothing but love and a listening ear when the darkness descended. You hand-wrote lines from John O'Donohue I needed to hear, which appear in Part Three of this book. In you, God sent me a friend I needed.

Equally, I mention with special love and affection Carol Roberts, my wife's roommate at Vanderbilt and her deep Christian friend. You were present when Elizabeth woke up in a Paris transplant hospital. You flew out to the ICU in South Carolina to be with Elizabeth as she was dying, bathing her and getting her ready to go home to the Lord she loved and wanting her to be at her precious best when I arrived from France to say what would be our final goodbye.

Eddie and Judy Parish helped me in the first years of my loss. I write to process, and they read to love and to understand. Bonnie Gorscak is a specialist in complicated grief and trauma. I wrote Part Three in the context of working with her. Thank you, Bonnie.

Job had poor friends. I have good ones. I thank God for you all.

Elizabeth is the love of God's heart pored into my life for which I am forever grateful. This book is my effort to say I love you, now on another shore in eternal light and life that Jesus Christ won for us. And alive in my heart of hearts.

Part One

A Life Lived Well in France

Preface

I HAVE CHOSEN THE title *Le Grand Voyage* for the story you will read. The French title has an obvious English equivalent, meaning the same thing. The story to be told takes place in France, and France is essential to its telling, as I trust you will come to understand.

The title is also chosen because it is paired in a famous ballad of the 60s, by Jacques Brel, with *notre Grand Amour*—our Grand Love, a love unfolding in the grand voyage of life. You will be reading about a grand love.

The subtitle is meant to serve as a loose rubric: *Life, Loss, Love*. At the heart of the grand voyage will be a struggle with the loss of a grand love: almost; then miraculously no; and then really.

I want to say in this telling, however, that loss is not the last word, and cannot be when one speaks truly about *un grand amour, notre grand amour*. So, the order in the subtitle is important.

I first tell the story of a life lived well in France. Life, then, is first. Loss is second. Love, crucially, is last. And love, being last, means the grand voyage never has a conclusion in the usual sense of storytelling. In the usual sense of life as we understand it.

I have written many books over the course of my life. They have a beginning, middle, and end, as do all stories, generally speaking. Everyone knows as they read along when they are getting to the conclusion and there is either satisfaction at what has unfolded and drawn to a close, or at times, relief. Also, the material form of a book you are holding, with its size and table of contents, regulates the way we speak about beginning, middling, and ending, and governs our expectations about "where we are."

To tell a story of great love on a great voyage means journeying alongside a great mystery. Great love has no conclusion. It surmounts and overcomes all loss, even, perhaps particularly, traumatic loss. There are reasons for this, and I will probe them in the course of the book, particularly in the third and final section. The book has a material form that the lived story cannot be contained by. Being robbed suddenly of a grand love leaves one in a place outside of time and the normal business of its unfolding.

What all this requires is the cultivation of memory. We live our lives without the fact of death presenting itself to us and asking us to consider the preciousness of moments as we pass through them, its mass and density bending and refracting the light so we can glimpse those moments afresh in their—shall we call it—eternal significance and depth. To try to do that would amount to a kind of insanity, even as we all know, more generally, what it means to be aware of the preciousness of our shared lives with those we love as we pass through life day-by-day.

To place love last, after life and loss, means to be given eyes to see the inner significance of life as it grows and illumines, revealing its deep beauty and truth, after death and the loss of a *grand amour*.

Cultivation of memory is itself a mystery embedded in what it means for us to live in time, under the providence of God, in whose hands time resides. Time participating, in ways hard at times to fully grasp on the voyage of life, in what we call eternal life, larger life, ages of ages, *siècles des siècles*.

Memory cultivated isn't following any obvious linearity. To "look back" isn't a tidy affair, arising from the clock face. The closest analogy might be that place of night talking we lodge under the word "dream." The dream. The past rising up as we sleep, bursts of random talking and seeing fighting to find narrative form, a story to be told, or the story that seeks to tell itself.

Under the title "dreams" we also have the nightmare, the talking and seeing that is fearful and scary. *Le grand voyage* consists of this dimension as well, though not in exaggerated and grotesque, deformed reality, but in the reality as it comes to us in lives we live through time, all of them finally ending in death.

From what I have said thus far, however, we may not say that the grand journey of life, ending in death, ours and those we love, conforms so clearly to the language of "finally ending." Or that is what I will endeavor to say in the book that unfolds before you here.

I allow life to be lived as I experienced it with Elizabeth, my *grand amour*, in one "sample year" in time, when we moved to France in 2015.

I did not write that story in the form of a contemporary "diary" account. I wrote about this life after loss. Indeed, several years after her death. It arose before me as I took its measure through the vehicle of memory. I wanted to recall a life that, in accordance with what I say above, took on a deeper character than one could have appreciated at the time.

That shows us the limits of our march through time when we are marching at the time.

It shows us that time as we march along cannot reveal its depth until confronted with, set alongside, what we struggle to understand as eternity in God. And that cannot be understood until we are changed by death and by loss. Especially the loss of a *grand amour*. Death and loss change us.

What is at question is whether they can give us eyes to see things more clearly. And that includes ourselves to start with, who will be seeking to see the *grand amour* on the grand voyage *coram deo*.

It must be said here as well. The grandeur of love grows after loss because its true character, its full account of itself, can only be properly approached and grasped—I'm reluctant to use the word—when the loved one is grieved as gone, and the life shared returns in fuller appreciation and in greater love. Becoming the *grand amour* it was at the time but could not be fully seen and embraced in this larger sense until placed in the hands of God and his time.

I do not want to theologize in this story. Fear not. The story carries its own reality and truth-telling capacity. It is rich beyond measure, because it enters what the psalmist calls "the jaws of death."

As a theologian, I have had to find new language to speak of *le grand voyage*.

But if I had one text that speaks into what I am saying in this preface, and in this book, it would be: "I tell you the solemn truth, unless a kernel of wheat falls into the ground and dies, it remains a single kernel; but if it dies it produces a great harvest" (John 12:24).

A Great Harvest. A *Grand Amour. Le Grand Voyage.*

1

Braque Bonjour

ELIZABETH AND I WERE sitting in a cozy café in Fontainebleau. It is a cozy town, especially when light with tourists. She's been to Versailles more often than I have, but we have both been there enough to know Fontainebleau feels much more authentic, drenched in long history, and just real. One can easily imagine Napoleon—himself late on the scene—waving from the famed horseshoe staircase, soon to be making his way to the Island of Elba. The "Court of Adieu."

My wife runs a French travel, language, culture business for niche clients. We were in Fontainebleau for a reason I don't now recall. We had taken the TRE commuter train down from Paris and were now enjoying a lovely lunch at a crowded but quiet café. My memory is of us just winding down from a busy season of our life, happy to be losing track of time in the Department of Seine et Marne, an hour south of Paris.

Blood pressure and life pressure abating, feeling ourselves breathing more calmly, eyes glistening from a white Burgundy from Beaune and contented stomachs, I see a man making his way out, carving his way through tables toward the door. Handsome, relaxed, accompanied by a very strong and confident dog on a leash. Dark black muzzle, posture alert, eyes happy, sixty-five pounds of muscle and attention, a coat of riotous black spots (*des taches*, in French). My left hand and his strong head gave me no choice but to ask the owner, as he passed by, if I could say hello. "What kind of breed is he?"

I had owned pointing dogs and I knew he was that for sure. The French word is *costeau*—sturdy. Chest dominant, balanced. Solid nose for spotting game in the brush. Sure of himself, and so content and self-contained.

His master declared in French, "Why, he is a Braque d'Auvergne. A Blue," he added. "Feel free to say hello."

The dog's super soft ears and happy eyes melted the hearts of Elizabeth and me. The Bleu d'Auvergne, I would learn, is so called because the central Massif region of France, known for its dormant volcanos and Blue Cheese, is the Auvergne. To "Braquer" is to point (or, to rob a bank). The Braque Allemand is a German Shorthaired Pointer. Braque Hongrie, Visla. And so on. He is called a Blue because his strong spottled body looks like blue cheese, Bleu d'Auvergne.

I thanked him, he could tell I admired his dog, and the two of them proudly marched forward to the door.

I turned to Elizabeth. She was smiling. Happy. Knew what was on my mind and agreed. "We will get a Braque d'Auvergne when we move here." And, so, we would.

Finishing our lovely lunch and spilling out onto the streets of Fontainebleau, we made our way to the Hotel l'Aigle Noir to let our lunch settle. A French dog would make our life complete. The sixteenth-century fireplace in the life we would share, next to a twelfth-century parish church, with its massive ramparts and pleasantly interrupting Angelus bells, would be where Marcel would lie and warm his sturdy frame. "Le Presbytère," 7 rue du petit Paris, Courances, twenty minutes from that lunch spot, on a road built by Field General Montgomery after the war, would be our home. A Braque d'Auvergne, our faithful companion.

2

The Wedding Hat

ELIZABETH WORKED FOR A family in Paris as a young girl, a sort of *aide de famille*. A lovely couple, him an American lawyer in London with a business residence in Paris, she British. Two young children. They lived on rue Saint Dominique in the seventh, just next to the neo-Gothic church St. Clothilde (where César Franck had been the organist). A four bedroom (rent-controlled) top floor flat, with a *chambre de bonne* under the roof, as is typical of these residences in Paris.

Their daughter was now grown up and getting married at the chateau of Bourron-Marlotte. The couple Elizabeth worked with also had a getaway home in said village, south of Fontainebleau on the commuter train line that loops south and then west, after the stop in Fontainebleau. The girl had been a keen equestrian, and Elizabeth accompanied them to this lovely rural retreat when they headed there to leave London and Paris business work behind.

When we were looking at places to rent in France, visiting the one that would be our home in Courances, we decided to spend a few days at the chateau in Bourron, which had been redone and was accommodating guests. This was to be where the wedding reception would be celebrated, after a wedding at the parish church in the charming village. Elizabeth was always on the lookout, as well, for possible venues for her travel clients. She relived her days going down there with the family she adored and whose children she was helping to raise.

When the invitation came for the now grown-up daughter's nuptials, off Elizabeth went to find an outfit and the requisite hat to accompany her choice. And off we went to Paris by flight from Dallas.

We know the routine very well, the lounges, customs routines, baggage claim and distances when on the ground. Our checked luggage—we would stay for a few weeks—and Elizabeth with hatbox in her lap, giddy with excitement to be seeing her adult charge now a grown woman, the village of her young years, the couple who had become very close friends (they crossed the Atlantic for our wedding in Dallas), and rejoice at her wedding. The kind of magical return to a life once lived, across the Atlantic, in a small village, as a young girl, reading French books to children, soon to be attending university herself and becoming a PhD graduate in French.

We had arranged for a driver who would take us to the hotel where we were staying in Fontainebleau. It was a beautiful day awaiting us in Paris as we touched down. If a bit hot, it certainly wasn't Dallas.

Our driver was there with his sign to pick us up. On reflection, the arrival area seemed a bit quiet, unlike the usual busy taxi drivers scampering for fares as passengers spill out with their luggage. There he was, alone, no other hired drivers alongside him with upheld signs in their two hands.

With a note of concern but encouragement as well, he said the country was on a strike due to conflict over the newly appearing Uber competition. There is a longer story here, but the gist was that his was the only car in the carpark. Our flight was early enough in the day that he had been able to get to the airport without hassle. The question was, would we be able to leave?

He put our bags in the car, and we took our seats, Elizabeth worried, precious hatbox in lap.

There was cause for concern, as it turned out. We came up the familiar ramp to get onto ground level, and it was blocked with luggage carts. Not good. I offered to get out and move them, and turning around to look at us both, his face telling a story, he said, No. That will not work. Will incite the taxi drivers ahead. Thronging the airport lanes on foot, burning tires, worked up into strike fury, and so forth.

He got out and offered to one growling taxi man that he was not Uber. A private driver. Here's my card and papers. Guests from the US, headed to Fontainebleau, his home, not Paris. Wan smile. It was not going to happen.

We sat in perplexity. He said, let me try to reverse and go out another way. We must have moved one foot and upon seeing this, twenty men hustled to the rear of the car to block that stratagem. Now they were getting worked up. The windows were lowered due to the heat and just to feel less trapped mentally. Arms reached in to grab water bottles and opening them, dashed water at us like so many harpies gone into frenzy.

Blocked front and back, the driver offered this proposal: Let me go in and change my clothes from my driver's uniform. Maybe I'll just look like a private citizen who happened to be in the wrong place. OK.

But that plot was foiled too. He shrugged, I did all I could, shook my hand, and deposited our bags on the curb.

Hatbox under her arm, I went off for a luggage cart. Now what awaited us was an entire Charles de Gaul airport in the same situation as us without any way to get into Paris by taxi transportation. The train ticket area was awash, to the sidewalls, with people, trying to buy tickets. Now including us.

I don't recall the details. Probably too irritating. But at last we were on board the RER headed to Paris. And of course, we would have to change and then catch the TRE to Fontainebleau.

I have never seen a train car so crowded. People sitting on the luggage in the aisle, every seat taken. People sitting on top of people sitting in the aisle. I'm not sure how we got a seat, but we did, crunched in on either side. Now it was getting hot, body heat plus outdoor heat, every window open.

Across from us sat a hapless young couple. Obviously not French. When we inquired about them—it was hard not to talk in such a crowded situation—they broke into smiles. "We're on our honeymoon." Somehow, when truly in love, it will all turn out OK. They looked each other in the eyes and you knew it was true.

Traversing the complicated system for getting from Gare du Nord to Gare de Lyon, at last we were on the train to Fontainebleau, and a grade up and less crowded than the cattle car from Roissy to Paris. A thought occurred to my ever-resourceful and just-damn-smart wife (a professional traveler). Chris, we've got to get from the station in Fontainebleau to the hotel, and as you know, that's not a short walk. There is no taxi service. I'll call the same transport company.

Positive news. They would have a driver meet us at the station to take us to the hotel. We needed a break from the bizarre morning we had just endured, four hours since touch-down.

Fontainebleau station is in the village next door, called Avon. Happy to have our feet on the solid ground of the station platform, I pulled the bags down breathing a sigh of relief. Elizabeth with her hatbox.

Up rushing to greet us was the driver. We smiled.

It was the same man who had come to pick us up at CDG airport. He had gotten home ahead of us. Hatbox in her lap, happy to be "home" ourselves, we headed off to our hotel.

3

Le Camino

"The Camino" refers, of course, to the famous pilgrimage trail, walked by countless pilgrims each year, to Santiago de Compostela, close to the Atlantic coast of Northern Spain. It is held to be the burial place of St. James the Apostle. Its distance away from normal paths of life probably helps lend to it exotic character and popularity. Far-flung, challenging, a route able to be picked at various points along the way, but all the same: whether close or far from the final destination, one is a Pilgrim on the Camino.

In fact, there are manifold "camino." One headed north from Portugal. One skirting across the bottom of France from Italy. Four major routes in France for pilgrims, from mediaeval times, spilling into this single country from all countries in Europe and Scandinavia. The best known one perhaps associated with Vézelay in Burgundy, the Basilica where Bernard of Clairvaux preached the second crusade.

And the paths of our own lives crisscross and double back and find their way to a common destination by many routes.

When I was a university student, I was fortunate to be asked to serve as a leader, along with two others, of groups going to Europe. Six weeks, twelve students, two VW camping buses. Crisscrossing Europe and meeting other groups and their leaders going counterclockwise to ourselves. Along with all the obvious major capitals in England and Europe, we had challenging physical adventures. Climbing the highest mountain in Austria, kayaking on the Danube, bicycling in the Netherlands, hot air ballooning in the Loire Valley, and running with the bulls at Pamplona. Yes, Hemingway was still holding students in his thrall.

I did trips two years in a row in summers in the late 70s. The tales about those trips could fill a book. Crossing the Iron Curtain into (the then) Czechoslovakia to visit the stunning Prague. Stomping over an icy glacier to snowy trails up to 3,800 meters with boots and crampons and sturdy Austrian guides.

All of those pilgrimage trails headed to Santiago converge in the enchanting village of St. Jean Pied du Port, in the Pyrenees.

Elizabeth and I were spending the first summer after our marriage in the Medoc, on the Atlantic coast of France. We were there for six weeks, in a gite (holiday lodging) outside the hamlet of Carcans. I was taking Sunday services for tourists and holidaymakers in the town of Soulac-sur-Mer, at the very top of this triangular region (Bordeaux on the east and the ocean on the west). The UNESCO heritage basilica there has the ominous name, Notre Dame de la fin des Terres, Our Lady of the End of the Lands. It has a famous lighthouse and on a clear day one can make out Royan to the north, below La Rochelle in the Department of Charente-Maritime across the Girande River.

All of this being due north of St. Jean Pied du Port, here too in the Medoc we have one of the four main pilgrimage routes in France headed south to Santiago.

So, three-and-a-half decades after my college "Camino" to the Pays Basque—to cross the Pyrenees at the famed Roncevaux (immortalized in the Chanson de Roland), and down to Pamplona for the running of the bulls—Elizabeth and I returned. In the car loaned to us for the summer, a lime-green Toyota station wagon, British drive (steering wheel on the right, left-hand shift), we carved our way through the vast Les Landes (formerly Gasgony) to the train station. I wanted to take the train again.

I had forgotten the lovely stews and omnipresent *pimente d'espelette* of Basque country. The charming train that chugs two slow hours up from Bayonne, below Biarritz. The bustling international charm, the excitement of pilgrims exchanging stories, the pelota courts, the unique admixture of Spain and France.

In 1978 we had descended from the valley pass (Roncevaux/Roncevalles in Spanish) about ninety minutes by VW bus down to the plain surrounding Pamplona. Those 90 hp vehicles, loaded with seven adults, luggage, even an electric guitar amplifier, gear strapped on the roof, have a top speed under the average Tour de France sprinter. We pitched our tents just outside of town alongside the Agra River. The fun had clearly already begun.

It was necessary to have those wanting to run sign release forms. Girls running, should they so choose, was not yet fully acceptable to locals, but the times were "a-changin," as Bob Dylan put it. We would rise early the next morning and head to the top of the barricaded streets where the bulls were held in enormous pens.

I had a Spanish teacher colleague at the prep school where I was teaching after college who happened to have grown up in Roncevalles. She had all the necessary insider knowledge, as her brothers had run with the bulls regularly. You want to be at the beginning of the run, she advised, not the middle. Running at top speed the bulls are very fast, will stick close to the rump ahead of them, and will steam past you if you stick to the rail. Amazing how tall they are as they rush by like tauros locomotives.

But for now, the day was for joining in the festival atmosphere. This included buying a *bota*, a Hemingway made-famous wine bag that had once upon a time been a sheep's bladder fitted with a nozzle. Now replaced with a manufactured version available at your local Pamplona *bota* shop. You head to the bar, elbow your way in, hand the bag to the barman, he fills it up with red wine, under a dollar for a liter. Behind the bar is the St. Fermin speciality, stacked like mini cordwood, reaching to the ceiling; in wax paper oozing with olive oil, hundreds of sandwiches on rough baguette-style bread, filled with a big fat egg omelet.

"I'll take two." One hundred pesatas.

I think of this now as we wander the streets of St. Jean Pied du Port, thirty-two years later, Elizabeth and me, on our own reminiscing *camino*. Turning down a lane, we find a charming espadrille store. Actually, it is a small atelier where Madame makes the popular, timeless footwear. Pulling aside the curtain, she proudly shows us the work area. In the sales part of the store, stacked like those egg omelet sandwiches, each in their own niche according to size and style, was a wall of espadrilles, bursting with color and good taste. (Now outfitted with soles other than rope.) Elizabeth, they are so inexpensive, go ahead and get a bunch of them.

We stayed in a charming cottage on the main street. Ate well. Did some hill climbing. Enjoyed the altitude. Memories of early days of my life, just as Elizabeth recalled hers in the small village south of Fontainebleau. The pilgrimage trails of our life. Converging at St. Jean Pied du Port.

France has forty different countries inside her borders, the Pays Basque being one of them. We will return to the Medoc in chapters to follow.

4

La Halte du Temps

WE HAD MOVED INTO our new house in the village of Courances. Its boulangerie and nearby market town were now well known. Our goods from the US had arrived. The house had been painted and a new kitchen put in. My office, in one of the outbuildings, was soon to follow. Elizabeth's gardening passion re-commenced. The Angelus rang in our mornings. It was time to get a puppy!

I have had hunting dogs and for me the main thing is getting first pick. There were five or six breeding kennels (*elévage*) in France for our new favorite breed, the Braque d'Auvergne. France being the size of Texas, I was not concerned about distance but instead the timing of mom's birthing schedule. We located a kennel to the south of Toulouse, on the border of the Ariège and Haute-Garonne departments, whose nearest town with accommodations was the charming sounding Montesquieu-Volvestre.

This is not a trip location for French Affaires, Elizabeth's travel company. The nearest known quantity for us was Cahors, not far from where we went on our honeymoon in the Lot/Perigord Noir region, the Dordogne region, as it is commonly known ("the river with a thousand castles").

The best thing about French Affaires is you have every excuse to travel to places in France you have not been. "We're doing research" covers every whim, every desire to learn about a new place on the map, every slight feeling of the need for an adventure. Elizabeth and I share a love of maps. We probably have a hundred road maps and fifty ordinance maps for trail walking. Where is Toulouse? What is there? How long will it take and down which autoroute? What is the Ariège known for?

The bulk of the seven-hour journey is on the A-20. Vierzon, Chateauroux, Limoges, Brive le Gaillard, not your most enchanting trajectory. We had bought a VW Passat station wagon (diesel). It came with a super back area that would become the new travelling home of our dog-to-come, as we would ferry him all across France. "Him," in that we agreed we wanted a male puppy.

Trip number one was to meet the breeder, and she us, and see the four-week-old puppies (tired mom had nine!). We had spoken on the phone several times and been given the details of how she would operate upon arrival. We found an accommodation in Montesquieu-Volvestre online and were delighted that this would be the place she would also recommend. It was a *chambre d'hôte*. That is, the owner of the house had rooms to book, with meals to be taken there with the owners. *La Halte du Temps* looked charming at the internet site. A seventeenth-century manor house in a bastide town.

A bastide is a fortified town laid out on a geometric grid, typically from the early Middle Ages. One is witnessing the rise of a genuine mercantile class, defensive of its status as such. Travelers know that these bastide towns can be found in certain regions of France (I think of the famous bastide towns south of the Dorgogne, but equally elsewhere.) Mercantilism can also be aligned with Protestantism of a later period (sixteenth century).

Well, we had never stayed at a *chambre d'hôte*, but it looked charming and there wasn't a lot to choose from. We were headed to a remote region. Good. I rubbed my hands in glee. New breed, new region, rural and a bit rough, off the beaten track. There we would find our new companion.

Off we left early in the morning, excited by the adventure. What is not to like? France awaits and a French dog awaits. I drive. Elizabeth hands me the credit card for the péage stations, pockets the paper receipts, and tells me when to stop *à faire peepee* (pit-stop).

I know the route quite well now, as I write this. It's how you get down to the Dordogne, a popular place for French Affaires travel, where I would come down to join Elizabeth and keep her company: eat and drink wine and enjoy the guests, all the hard work having been done by my sweet wife.

Hi, girl! I'm here. Let's have a bit of our fun now.

A dull route but also one on which you can make good time. The French have a slightly vulgar expression that one associates with several of the places on the A-20. "Back of beyond" is a cleaned-up version of a phrase having to do with the anatomy of the backside.

Well, we are motoring along well. Making good time. Should be at our lodging in time to wind down and get an *apéro* at our new destination: see the bastide town, stroll along the charming Arize river, visit the historic church. The A-20 route is free of traffic and we are clocking the miles.

About forty-five miles north of Toulouse is Montauban where the A-20 gives way to the A-62. It in turn forms a peripheral road around this sizeable town of about half-a-million citizens. Passing by Montauban, suddenly our lovely pace of travel came to a dead halt. I mean, dead halt. Slow enough for people to get out of their cars, every now and then, to gawk and scratch their heads or tighten their fists. The latter knew what was going on. Yes, a strike. The omnipresent "manifestation," "la grève," as at the Paris Airport.

The French strike about anything and everything, as is commonly known. To the chagrin and puzzlement of outsiders. It's a kind of national sport or pastime. We turned on the radio and yes, a strike was announced for the motorway around Toulouse. Isn't that nice. They also actually tell you when they are going to ruin your trip, a trip, mind you, you have been paying for since the first pay station south of Paris. No matter.

We had seen this kind of activity before, in general terms, on the highways. Truck drivers showing their support for the strike du jour somewhere else in the country, slowing down to annoy you for a couple of miles. But this was our first experience with the "operation escargot." It means what is says on the tin. Truck drivers (*poid lourd*—eighteen-wheelers as we say) get athwart each other, straddling lanes, four abreast on three lanes so no one can pass, and they drive at five miles per hour, or slower, depending on how much they're enjoying it, or due to orders from command central for today's strike. I think it took us two hours to go about ten miles. My mind remains unclear from vestigial rage.

When you finally get to the place where they let you go by, there is a charming group of strikers smoking cigarettes, joking, burning tires if restless, waving you by as if they are in charge of nuclear codes or just generous enough to not hold you up another five hours—you may thank us. I was thinking how if you tried to pull this in the US, especially after having handed over about a hundred dollars to travel on the road in the first place, your average polite Texan would pull out a gun and shoot the man waving you through with a cigarette in his mouth and a smile on his face.

We are not doing that anymore, thank you very much.

The phrase *La Halte du Temps*, the ever so charming name of our *chambre d'hôte*, means "A Halt in Time." This damn Toulouse stoppage was not what we had in mind with that expression. After you have been moving along at under five miles per hour, you can't help but hit the accelerator. And for all I know they turn off the speed cameras after having asked paying drivers to crawl behind truck drivers who are out to "operation escargot" your trip.

Fortunately, we did not have far to go. We were ready to arrive and have a glass of wine or something stronger.

5

An Evening to Remember

Having passed the strike gauntlet, an hour remained to the *chambre d'hôte, La Halte du Temps*. We went straight there to book in and get settled. The seven-hour trip had become ten hours and now it was about 6 p.m. A nice woman greeted us and gave me instructions about where to park the car. Our few bags were deposited, and I went off to park the VW wagon. Elizabeth speaks fluent French and is good at small talk—not easy until your language skill is good, and your ear for accents accustomed to that next higher gear.

I returned and was directed to the room. We asked for a bottle of wine, which she brought up, along with a *tire-bouchon* (corkscrew; *bouchon* also means traffic jam, so appropriate).

The manor house was large, and the rooms very nice. We would learn that Madame's father had been a professor at the University of Toulouse, and this was the family home. The furnishings we assumed were typical of the Ariège and Haute-Garonne region (Garonne is the main river that traverses Toulouse, its capital).

We were bushed and a bit knackered by the annoying slow down. A glass of wine was putting that right. Madame had said dinner was at 8. She would see us downstairs. We would eat in the kitchen area, which had us assuming we might be the only guests.

We tidied up for a much-anticipated dinner, our stomachs growling. Making our way down the creaking staircase, we realized we had no idea where the kitchen actually was. I knocked and opened one door tentatively. It was her father's study. Books on floor-to-ceiling book shelves. As an academic, I tried to guess his subject area but moved along on our search. No, not here. Then, at last a door that opened on what was obviously a kitchen. A table set for four.

A huge open-cooking fireplace, such as one would use in the seventeenth century, dominated the cozy *piece*. A roaring fire carried us back into that century and manner of life. Now, where was Madame? We called out *coucou*. She was a warm-hearted woman in bearing, and not at all formal. In about an hour, we would be on *tutoyer* terms (the familiar "you").

Je suis ici! Here I am, her kindly voice called out. Obviously, the former kitchen, now a dining area, meant there was a modern kitchen. We passed through a half-open door into a very nice preparation and kitchen area. She was, after all, running a business. The website showed us a well-stocked area for *petit-dejeuner*, when the season would be bringing guests to the region known for hiking, fishing, and all things rural. It was a region known as well for *elévage*: dogs, cats, bees, orchards, trout, you name it. When we would take the fifteen-minute drive to the breeding kennel, the winding roads and general landscape reminded me of West Virginia. "Wild, wonderful" as the ad campaign put it.

She assured us dinner was on the way. We chatted a bit, and she suggested we sit and stay warm (it was February) next to the fireplace. She handed me a bottle of red and a *tire-bouchon*. She'd be with us shortly. *Volontiers* (you bet) we replied. I was happy to return and sit in the cozy dining area. Elizabeth was wearing one of her (and my) favorite outfits and her face was happy, glowing. This is why she and I moved to France.

We couldn't help but notice that the grand table was set for four. Probably another guest we had not encountered (or whose room we had not stumbled into). This was our first *chambre d'hôte* experience and we were loving it. What a nice idea, especially if you own a big seventeenth-century manor house in such a charming part of France, off the beaten trail.

In came the starter, Madame closing the door with her bottom, removing her *tablier* (apron), tray placed on the sideboard. I don't recall what we ate that night, except that it was beyond exceptional. Perhaps a trout starter, I know it was a hearty beef or pork main dish, and I recall a superb accompanying sauce. The very special desserts sumptuously fruit-filled, and not at all heavy.

But I am jumping the gun a little. Elizabeth and I exchanged glances. She was across the table from me, and Madame to my left. The empty chair, with a setting like ours at the ready, was to my right. It was not our business to ask, and Madame acted as if this was terribly normal. The first bottle of wine was doing its work. Madame clearly knew her routine, which meant she could relax, and we could talk.

I relive this experience now, able to speak flowing French myself, after being immersed in situations just like this, and a lot of mental elbow grease expended at language schools over our years in France. This is where it was a joy to be able to experience true French life to the full, because Elizabeth could easily pass as a native. Her French was *impeccable*.

We were learning about the region. About Madame's professor father. About her family history. About the house itself. She knew Arlette, who was the professional breeder of Barque d'Auvergne dogs at the Ruisseau Montbrun kennel in Daumazon-sur-Arize. Arlette sent her guests there from all over France, all wanting this special breed. And in our case, a couple from Texas now living in Courances next to its historic chateau.

Enjoying the conversation and moving at the usual French pace over our starter dish, *pop*, the door to my right opened and, voila, the mystery guest had arrived. He did not look like a guest, but rather someone taking his customary place at the head, across from Madame. About her age. He said excuse me and tucked into the dish now placed before him.

Now this will be fun, I thought.

He was not averse to speaking and the conversation picked up, the fireplace and wine bringing much atmosphere and a lively feel of joy. He looked a bit rough, though obviously with high intellect. He was, as we would learn, a *soixante-huitard*—literally, a sixty-eighter, the year 1968 being the year of all the famous Paris student demonstrations. I suppose he was what we would call a hippy, now about five years my senior. He smiled proudly in letting us in on his lineage and status.

Unlike Madame, he was from Paris. The Ariège was the place to come to live the free and real life. Back to nature. Live off the land. Woodstock. Break away from convention and formality. The University of Toulouse also had this same free spirit.

He had come down here to raise bees. The land and housing were cheap and easy to acquire on the properly rebellious *soixante-huitard* savings.

The main dish arrived. Madame offered her commentary at intervals. They were clearly a couple. We opened the next red. This was fun. Elizabeth glowed across from me, my back to the fireplace. He would rise and come back with a fresh load of wood from time to time. The meat dish—perhaps a local stew—was fortifying. Brilliant accompanying dishes passed by as needed. We were guests in the home and hearth of two true locals. He had not left this rural area from the moment of his arrival, now forty-plus years on.

The bee business was getting off the ground and he was "living off the land." Then he got stung and was so ill the ambulance had to be called. Deathly allergic to bee stings. He put away his smoker and exotic suit, sold the business, and nursed his wounded ego. Plans crashing down.

Instead, however, he trained himself to be a fresco painter, got good at it, in time was contacted by Madame to do some refurbishing work for her, and the rest is history.

We talked about all kinds of things that evening. A third bottle went around. Dessert and the local *marc* (fruit or flower Brandy—reminded me of Bavarian schnapps). Fire restoked. Now past midnight. The operation escargot a blur in the rear-view mirror. We were indeed experiencing *La Halte du Temps.* A moment rich and rare. Clear in my mind even today. My happy and beautiful wife, reveling in her command of French and me keeping up not too badly.

I did ask what we were to make of the strike we just experienced, and Monsieur said, it's just a *grève stérile.* A sort of gesture, meant to remind the public at large that sympathy for the worker is necessary. Did it make sense? Was it productive? No, a sterile strike. Why didn't people object? It's a part of being French. We don't do anything fast.

Like our evening, I thought to myself. A meal, good conversation, wine, a fireplace, a kindly couple happy to share their life with us.

This washes away the road grime and the fraught mind. We said thank you, *merci infiniment*, and arm and arm climbed the staircase, Madame and Monsieur waving to us from the door of our evening together.

Une Halte du Temps. Indeed.

6

Ruisseau Montbrun

We slept well. When it is so quiet, it almost feels like a sleep blanket has descended. We dressed and headed down for the *petit déjeuner*. Our appointment at the kennel was for 9.30. The drive would take us fifteen minutes.

Madame bustled about and saw to our being well taken care of. Monsieur had disappeared, as was his wont. We finished our breakfast and did a quick tour of the quaint bastide village, and a stroll along the river.

Thank goodness for the GPS. This was the land of small winding roads, unruly nature, various entrepreneurial ventures. We saw the sign for Ruisseau Montbrun Elévage and turned in. Arlette, the owner was at the ready. A small, vigorous, sturdy woman in her sixties, running a successful breeding kennel. Off we hustled to meet the puppies.

Her operation consisted of small whelping cabins, for lack of a better word. Cinder block, maybe a bit of paint to brighten things up, a chamber for the pups to clamber about, and mom's little quarters. There is nothing quite like this, a squirming bundle of puppies—nine in this case—looking like a moving mass of black and white energy. Black heads, four-week-old bodies full of mottled black markings, hard to separate. It is no wonder that as they grow up, it takes time for them to think of themselves apart from the moving mass that was their early start of life.

Those of you who have experienced this "pick a puppy" moment recall that each wee one has a differently colored little collar to be able to distinguish one from another. We wanted a male puppy, so that helped narrow things down a bit.

Elizabeth and I studied the boys. We were first in line so our choice would be secure. That said, Arlette knew that they were still growing up, and so we were able to pick out our two favorites, and she would let us know more about each one's personality in the coming weeks. We were not allowed to hold them or touch them.

She entered the little playground, giving tired mom a pat, and extracted the one we first identified. She would come to the door (one of those doors that divide in half with the bottom fixed and the top open) and hold up the little guy. We got a good look, and then she returned him to the puppy heap and brought the second one we picked out for us to eyeball.

It would be taupe collar and wine-colored collar. Our top choices. Nameless for now.

In France (and I believe other European countries) dogs and horses receive a name according to the year in which they are born. This helps identify their age. 2016 was the year of "M." 2017 "N" and you get the picture. We would give our puppy a name that started with "M."

We had discussed all the other relevant details with Arlette on the phone and would be checking in with her as they got their next round of shots (which is why we were not to touch them) and other puppy details. Their little tails had been docked to breed standard already.

The purpose of our journey completed, our car already packed, our goodbyes at *La Halte du Temps* warmly relayed after breakfast, it was back to Courances, eight hours—we hoped!—up the autoroute. Fortunately, no *operation escargot* hindered our return trip. You can only annoy the general public so long, or they will turn against you and withdraw their sympathy, such as it is.

We made good time. Made mental notes about our new "M" puppy, comparing the two we had selected. Thought of names. Took note of places we might stay upon return. St. Cirq Lapopie is one of the famous "les plus beaux villages en France" sites. We were already thinking about ways to avoid Toulouse, and to do the puppy swap four weeks later, around Montauban, north of the capital. This time we would make a stop at a charming village and take it in.

More "French Affaires research" as we would say.

We arrived, turned the ancient key on our wooden gate, entered our courtyard, and felt the peace descend. The huge church ramparts a kind of bulwark against all foes, nestled on our flank, guarding our lives. We were home, Le Presbytère, 7 rue du Petit Paris, Courances.

7

Our Home in France

7 Rue du Petit Paris

ELIZABETH AND I MOVED to France full-time in late 2015. We married later in life, both of us single and for the first time. The odds of that are hard to believe. I was mid-fifties, she ten years younger. On the other hand, we had led busy professional lives, were independent, had travelled a good deal, and that set us up to give thanks for finding each other. A true gift of God.

I had lived in Scotland for a decade, a professor at the University of St. Andrews, having grown tired, restless of Yale and New Haven, Connecticut. The University of Munich had been the next stop in route to a PhD at Yale (followed by a tenured faculty position). German was an essential research language and I enrolled at Goethe Institute and started formal graduate studies there. Language teaching is a central aspect of my career. A third of my adult life had been spent abroad when I took Elizabeth out for drinks in Dallas. When she spoke French, my heart was moved. A life shared in Europe might await us.

At the time, I was teaching at the University of Toronto, a post that allowed me to work only with PhD students, and not to have to live full time in residence. I came back from Scotland and moved to Dallas, where I had a position as theologian in residence for the Episcopal Diocese, and on the staff at a large urban parish church. I met Elizabeth there. She had grown up in Highland Park, Dallas. After our marriage, we bought a house in the nearby Preston Hollow neighborhood.

I am getting ahead of myself in that we courted for a year. After those first shared glasses of wine—and an Armagnac night-cap—it would be constant time together, and a trip to France planned almost immediately. We flew to Paris and stayed at her favorite hotel and took the fast train (TGV) to Les Baux-de-Provence, a place we would return to almost annually. We celebrated Palm Sunday in Maussane-les-Alpilles, with local olive branches in our hands instead of palms.

Elizabeth had been a French professor and then entered corporate life, traveling internationally for Texas Instruments and Dell. Her dream was to share France with Americans. When we met, she started French Affaires, LLC, a niche travel, culture, and language business. Dallas is a superb place for intelligent traveling clients, and she was well-known in the city.

Elizabeth was a sought-after lecturer, teacher, purveyor of an infectious love of France. She organized a French cookbook club and a "Tour de France" lecture series, complete with regional dishes and drinks corresponding to where the "Tour" was. Voila, the joy of France without *décalage horaire* (jet lag).

I was thrilled that she was getting to live her dream.

And that I would get to share it alongside her. It was time for fun for us both.

Her business blossomed and came to full flower in those years (2008–15). Six trips a year, to all regions, would come in due course. Normandy, Loire Valley, Dordogne, Côte d'Azur, Burgundy, Provence, Corsica, and of course Paris, where she had spent so much of her younger life.

Living in France would make the travel demands and running the business much easier. I already had a flexible academic arrangement, allowing me to be resident for intensive term seminars in Toronto and in time, of course, the distance learning formats, when COVID invaded our lives. Much of PhD supervision is at the writing phase of students' careers, once coursework, comprehensive exams, and a dissertation colloquium were completed. I had been teaching at Yale and St. Andrews for going on twenty-five years, so these routines were familiar to me in my Toronto post.

I am also an ordained priest in the Episcopal/Anglican church, with church work over the years in Germany, Scotland, Canada, and the United States. I saw a third-time post advertised in the Church of England's Diocese in Europe, in Fontainebleau, interviewed and was called.

During this time, we were already crisscrossing France for pleasure or for Elizabeth's business. She was taking the Garden Club of Dallas group on a famous gardens tour, from Paris and down to the Loire Valley in 2015. I was in the area, and we had already begun to look at houses to rent for our much-anticipated France sojourn. Elizabeth knew the manager at the chateau of Courances, one of the stops for the Garden Club trip. The chateau owned houses in Courances and in the nearby village of Fleury-en-Biere, where a sister chateau owned by the de Ganay family was located. The former rectory of the village church had come into the possession of the Marquis de Ganay, who had also been the mayor of this three-hundred-person village an hour south of Paris.

Elizabeth had been shown around by Patrick Deedes, the man in charge of administration and promotional activities at the chateau. The house needed work, but had, as Elizabeth liked to say, "good bones." One can only intuit so much from photos sent to us via the internet by Patrick, and I also wanted to take a look. The setting was hard to beat. The rectory and the church next door reminded me much of my life growing up, the son of a parish priest and then school chaplain and headmaster. When the Angelus bells rang from the *cloche*, the bell tower hovering over the property below, I was transported to another time. The village life, the chateau grounds, the small cemetery honoring allied airmen shot down in the Second World War, the forest trails that would become our dog's stomping grounds, full of pheasants and chukkers for him to chase—it was something magical.

Above all, there was the garden area, church ramparts as one side of the *cloture*, the walled enclosure that would be our oasis, with a *potager* and massive ceramic pots, from Ravel, and new tree plantings undertaken by Elizabeth. The Angelus sounded three times a day, as in the celebrated nineteenth-century painting by Francois Millet, of the Barbizon School, a village not fifteen minutes away.

Of course, we said yes, settled on a rental amount, and other details. A new kitchen would be installed, the house thoroughly prepared and painted, ancient *tomette* clay floor tiles replaced and buffed, chimneys cleaned, and a new office for me in one of the outbuildings (a new roof would be included and a wood stove and mezzanine for my desk).

We returned to Dallas and began the work of selling our house, putting things in storage, and readying items to be shipped by sea container to our new address. We popped our Mercedes sedan in last, as we figured we would need two cars.

In mid-December, as darkness fell, the moving van pulled away from our lovely home in Preston Hollow. We boarded a flight for France the following day. Our new life in France was beginning.

8

Pierres d'Histoire

We knew that it would take a good six weeks to do all the work on the house. As it turned out, the chateau was soon to be the home of a business venture associated with Pierres d'Histoire ("stones of history"). They are particularly active in the Isle de France area around Paris but have other projects in Normandy and across France. The idea is to take historical properties, restore them to a high quality, and then advertise them for holiday rental.

In the case of the chateau of Courances, the concept is a little different. The chateau in former times (it was built in 1630) had a good number of outbuildings associated with work taking place on the grounds. A mill. A cow milking barn. A workshop. A sawmill. A farm shop. These no longer active, the buildings had fallen into disrepair. They are all located within the grounds of the chateau and enclosed inside their gates. Pierres d'Histoire rightly saw their attractiveness as holiday cottages (*gites* in French) or small houses (as they like to call them).

There are also holiday lodgings run by them at the chateau of Fleury-en-Biere, walking distance from the chateau of Courances, and owned by the same de Ganay family. Only parts of that chateau presently inhabited, Pierres d'Histoire has chosen certain towers and other choice parts of the chateau to restore. Each setting has its unique features and offerings. In the case of Courances, guests have full access to the chateau grounds.

Elizabeth and I are frequent visitors to the Gardens of Eyrignac in the Perigord Noir (Southwest France) and know the charming owner. My wife is very pretty which gives her some unique advantages, paired with her intelligence and excellent French. I recall asking him what his favorite chateau and grounds were (apart from his own, of course). "Courances" he replied without hesitation.

There are no gardens at the chateau of Courances as one thinks of that. Rather, there are water gardens, of the genre one finds at Marquessac and Eyrignac in the Dordogne, for example, or Versailles and (close to my German ancestor's home) at Schloss Schwetzingen near Heidelberg. I am hardly an expert, though I have seen these water gardens regularly in travels across France.

What makes them unique, I believe, at Courances is their size, distribution, and the grandeur of the engineering feat. Not a single mechanized pump is involved, yet the water is constantly moving through a system of pools and long, grand canals. The largest at Courances was indeed a model for Versailles. There is a Japanese garden, a sort of *folie*, but apart from that—and it is charming, flanking the Pierres d'Histoire properties—Courances is known solely for the achievement of its water system and distribution of canals. It has remained a touch *sauvage*. Grand long alleys of trees. This would soon be our new dog's playground, and ours as well.

Arriving in December at the Paris airport, in the morning hours, it is still dark. People tend to forget that Paris lies on the same latitude as the forty-eighth parallel separating Canada from the United States. We went through customs, collected our luggage, found our way to the rental car area, and were given a nice sturdy station wagon. We knew our way to Courances, but this felt very, very special. We were beginning our new life in France. *C'est parti!*

At this time of the year, and early in the morning, and most importantly, not going into Paris, but rather to the Departments of Seine et Marne and Essonne, one can make reasonably good time. We are map people. The route can be tricky, and we thought to turn on the car's GPS as an *aide de route*. Only problem: What popped up was Korean (as best we could make out), and without knowing the language, one could not operate the buttons that would get us into English or French. We'd have time to do something about that, before buying our own (second) French car.

I can remember to this day the joy of arriving. You come down the A-6 and just before the pay station (*péage*) at Fleury-en-Biere, the exit reads Courances. If you know where to look, you can make out the long-running walls—crumbling here and there—of the chateau of Fleury. This would become our "coming back home" route for the years to come. Busy autoroute giving way to stubble fields, and forests, track roads, and walking trails that mark our arrival at the village of Courances.

You can see in the distance the church tower rising above the houses it surrounds, marking the place we will live for the next four years. The entrance road is marked with a high metal crucifix, with the body of Jesus doing his saving work.

We come to the small town square. There is the Mairie. Christmas is days away. The area is adorned with carefully wrapped packages telling Pére Noel we are here and ready for his visit. A light snow has fallen. It is still morning, and the small village is quiet.

The chateau dominates the village, once you get to the town square. The church, St. Etienne, is now on our left. Our home is being prepared. We have been told where to park, for the lodgings of Pierres d'Histoire are just behind the gate next to our new home at 7 rue du Petit Paris. We feel we are being tucked into seventeenth-century France, and that is because we are.

Patrick has stocked our new temporary home: preserves, milk, coffee, tea, wine; a handwritten note with directions to the boulangerie. He knew our arrival time.

I unload the luggage. We find the key to *le Moulin*, the Mill, and find we are alone among the four lodgings. We have the place to ourselves. It is dark, snow falling in light wind. I put on my Barbour coat and walk the seven minutes to the bakery. I know Elizabeth's favorite pastries. I add a warm baguette. I am excited to be in this special village, with my special wife, our Mill home, waterwheel slowly turning. Water coming to a boil for coffee.

I'll build a fire when we have eaten and have looked around our new home, checked out the two bedrooms, small work areas, fire up the internet, and settle in.

How nice that last phrase sounds.

9

La Serre

I THINK ONE OF the reasons a place like Le Moulin has such a deep, calming resonance is that it is fresh, has nothing familiar about it, is free of the goods of our accumulating lives. Elizabeth, me, three suitcases, the jackets we wore leaving Dallas and anticipating winter in France. The coffee press, the simple boulangerie, the quiet streets (*ruelles,* lanes), the snow freshly fallen on the chateau grounds, the paths to discover and walk. (We are in a veritable goldmine for *les sentiers balisés,* carefully marked trails mapped with charts you can buy at the bookstore.) The short days. The wood fire no different down the ages immemorable. Same with the church bells, now marking 8 a.m., noon, and 5 p.m.

I am back at my boarding school in Western North Carolina, where the Angelus rang at five o'clock and asked us to be quiet and stop where we were, until the final trolling peal. I'd like to say with the same downturned faces in prayer of the couple in the field of Millet's famous painting, but boys must grow up to be men. We were only starting that process.

Elizabeth gets to sleep late. I wasn't good at that. I love her lying in bed, the *grasse matinée* (sleep in), groggy and warm, slightly incoherent as sleep loses its place and we awake to a world dawning. We are not where we usually are, and so the daily chores and checklists and anxieties are lost in the ether.

Courances, we will learn, is made up of three sets of people. One-third is families living in smaller houses, some recently built in a new quarter (*a lotissement*). One-third is people with *residences secondaires* in this charming mediaeval village with its chateau and tolling bells, typically from Paris. One-third is *en retraite*—retired folks with means who have found a great place to buy a home and invite *les petits-enfants*. Total population, around three hundred.

So, it is quiet. Marvelously, rejuvenatingly still. No wonder Elizabeth sleeps so soundly.

This has sent my mind back to other experiences like this we have shared in France—before we moved here, and which conspired to make that happen.

I am a writer of various kinds of academic books. It comes with my position, and it is how one attracts graduate students anxious to work with a published scholar. I had been given a contract to write a commentary on one of Paul's letters. I was trying to move out of some familiar writing tracks—not unlike moving to Courances—and so accepted the invitation (my area of writing was Old Testament at the time). The commentary series was an experimental one, asking the authors to leave their favorite haunts and strike out. I resonate with that, by nature. I wanted to re-situate the single Letter to the Colossians within the larger corpus of letters attributed to Paul.

As noted above, I had come to a point in my professional career after full-time posts at Yale and St. Andrews—and now on *le grand voyage avec ma femme*—that I had been able to carve out my own rhythms: Elizabeth and me, fresh trails, adventures to be shared, husband and wife.

We had spent so many fun days in les Alpilles that we decided it would be our home and my writing atelier, for a two-month stretch. Elizabeth is wise about finding unique lodgings and she has many personal contacts to draw on. This is the region around St-Remy de Provence, to the west of Aix-en-Provence, where the grand alpine ranges, having descended as they move west, begin to find their ground-level resting place above Arles and east of the Gard. *Alpilles* meaning miniature alps.

So, our writing home, our relaxing home, our uncluttered-of-the-rush-and-bother home, in the middle of an olive grove, at the foot of Les Baux, appeared in the form of a two-month lease. *La Serre*, it was called.

A *serre* is a hothouse, a place for storing plants in the winter, among other things. It could be all glass, *une verrerie*, or as in our case, a building with lots of windows and sliding doors. *La Serre* had been converted into a charming two-bedroom cottage. We were in the middle of an olive orchard. The main house was at some distance, so we had total privacy. We would be there in late Spring through June, perfect months in les Alpilles.

Elizabeth had discovered the region taking clients to the Relais et Chateau hotel, le Cabre d'Or (the legendary "golden goat" in Provençal) and we were located about a football field away from some of the private independent properties on the road behind the main hotel. We had stayed there in 2009 after we first met, now seven years ago. The area (St-Remy-de-Provence, Maussane, Eygalières, Fontvielle, Paradou) is a fixture for French Affaires trips, and we know it and its locals well.

Les Baux de Provence is a rocky outcrop that is crowned with a ruined castle overlooking the plains to the south. Its name refers to its site—in Provençal, *bauç* is a rocky spur. From the village name the word bauxite was coined for aluminum ore when first discovered there in the early nineteenth century. If you know the stories of Marcel Pagnol (Jean de Florette and Manon des Sources), you may recall the young teacher searching the hills and discovering the muddy material used to block up the water source that would bring ruin to Jean. *C'est de la bauxite.*

In a twist of fate, the famous actor who played the evil mastermind, Daniel Auteuil (together with his uncle Caesar, played by Yves Montand), would later buy a property near Paradou. Le Bistrot Paradou is a hugely fun inn just west of Maussane. The fixed price includes all the wine you care to drink. I treasure a photo of Elizabeth and her driver Rémy standing next to the famous actor, he and my wife deep in conversation.

In fact, several well-known people have discovered the pleasant climate and (still for now) slow paced lifestyle of les Alpilles. Angelina Jolie and Brad Pitt bought a vineyard property outside of Eygalières. This is the land of Frederic Mistral and Vincent van Gogh. The latter, supported by his brother, lived in Arles—Gauguin and he had an ill-fated friendship there—before he was committed to the asylum at the *Monastère Saint Paul de Mausole*, just south of St-Remy. At Saint Paul, Van Gogh produced the majority of his paintings, including *Starry Night*. The nuns gave him a second room for an atelier to help calm his nerves and there he painted virtually non-stop.

We visit with clients annually and have a close friend from Van Gogh's village in the Brabant who has permission to paint where Vincent painted.

My writing routine involves long walks after lunch, after writing for several hours in the morning. I use this as a way to conceive what I will be writing next, then return to *la Serre*, and edit and write for another hour. I follow the rule of Hemingway. Never stop when you have concluded, but rather when you can easily pick up again. On the path up the hill beside *la Serre*, one passes by a private domain owned by Guns and Roses, or so the famous Paris DJ who is renting us this property tells me.

Further along that path, are grand quarries of bauxite, reddish caverns of the aluminum rich earth. Manon des Sources come alive!

Elizabeth is always busy with French Affaires and this is a perfect retreat for her. We go shopping, take walks of our own, visit friends at le Chateau des Alpilles, go to Mass, and visit all our favorite towns. We have vacationed here often and will return when we have settled into our new home.

The time passed quickly. When I have already done the research for a writing project, I can make very good progress.

La Serre is a hothouse where good memories are stored forever.

10

Noël 2015

We had arrived at our new home in France just before Christmas. How exciting. No duties for me this year! Fire roaring in the fireplace. Elizabeth cozy and happy, living her dream. We are getting to know Patrick and his wife and family who live a stone's throw away in another chateau property. He is originally from Zimbabwe, an Englishman whose life on an estate there made for beckoning him to the same manner of life here.

Patrick met his wife in Manhattan. Both worked for Ralph Lauren. Elizabeth had Googled her and upon seeing her face said she was the brunette model face for Ralph Lauren. Not my terrain.

That was now some years ago. She had left the busy New York lifestyle in exchange for raising a family and living in rural France. They now had three girls, one of them an accomplished polo competitor, like her father. Patrick would in time woo the *Fédération Nationale de Polo* to Courances, which had several superb grounds for the sport.

We would come to learn a bit more about his wife Isabelle, née Townsend. Her father had courted Princess Margaret, and they would pass weekends at Courances during this time. He was the famous Royal Air Force flying ace from World War Two and could buzz the two of them down to France from England after the war in his jaunty aircraft. We know him now from the series *The Crown*, which fortunately had not yet appeared during our time there. It was not a series that put her father in a flattering light. (I have not seen it.)

We went to Christmas Mass in what would be our church home in the nearby market town of Milly-la-Fôret, prior to my taking up duties as the Anglican chaplain in Fontainebleau. That would still be some months off, due to background checks. Having lived in the UK, Canada, and the US, agencies in these respective countries joined the FBI for security clearances. I was happy to have the time to enjoy our village and our neighbors.

There are several very nice restaurants in Milly. We enjoyed a lovely Christmas lunch there after church. The French would not understand a nice lunch at less than two hours, and at Christmas longer still. We nodded to faces we had seen in church who were dining there. They would become very close friends.

Milly, as it is called, was the home of Jean Cocteau, whose pleasant home and gardens are at the end of the lane across from the parish church. He did the mural paintings at a chapel on the outskirts of town, la Chapelle de Saint-Blaise des Simples. Saint-Blaise was renowned for healing miracles, associated with his knowledge of medicinal herbs, called "des simples." The parish church looking down on our home was named for St-Etienne, St. Stephen the martyr, a physician and during the Middle Ages revered as the saint known for healing miracles. The word "Courances" is likely associated in some way with the verb *courir*, to run, as in running or flowing water. The abundant spring water that fed the famous water gardens at the chateau also gave birth to the medicinal herbs of wide variety found in this region.

Christian Dior, the famous fashion designer, had a country retreat a short walk from our house, the Moulin de Coudret, complete with landing strip and a dozen bedrooms for guests. It had passed into the hands of a famous camera lens developer from Paris and was during our time in desuetude. But the memory of Dior was preserved in a perfume he created and named, well of course, "Milly la Fôret."

Patrick and Isabelle invited us over for drinks on New Years Day. Several of the other property renters (*locataires*) were present. The majority of these rental properties were on a single lane in Fleury-en-Biere, as noted above the sister chateau and only partially inhabited. It was fun to meet our new neighbors. I felt excited about our dawning new life and was also thrilled my wife could speak French like a local. Isabelle's father was born in Rangoon, Burma, and she had lived all over the world. She spoke excellent French, as did Patrick. They were raising their children at the international school in Fontainebleau, and they too were bilingual.

To stretch our legs on the unusually clear day, we decided on a long walk to Fleury. There are dedicated hiking trails linking the two chateaux villages, next to the forest track owned by the de Ganay family. One can also go through the woods, a favorite of our Braque d'Auvergne to come. It takes about ninety minutes. I walked with Isabelle and learned about her upbringing and her adventures, and her decision to leave Ralph Lauren to become a happy mom of three girls. She was now something of a free-spirited woman, dressing as she pleased, liberated from what must have been an intense life of clicking cameras and public over-exposure.

The days are short at this time of the year, but dusks are long. I had lived for nine years in Scotland and was familiar with sundown at 3:30 p.m. We too, Elizabeth and I, had been liberated from our life in the US, and were to become companions with these fascinating neighbors. The families in Fleury were from Paris. They came down to relax, ride, hunt, and just enjoy the change of pace. They had nothing to prove and were intent on slowing down and putting away the watch.

The Marquis of the chateau of Courances was no longer alive, though the aged Marquise was often in residence in her lodgings on the top floor. Her husband had been the mayor of the small village. By stratagems I no longer recall the specifics of, he had found a way to preserve a sort of carve-out in this region but fifty minutes from Paris. The train lines passed to the east (Fontainebleau) and to the west of us (a slow commuter train, or RER, with sixteen stops to Gare de Lyon). You would not pop on a train to come to Courances or Fleury. It was like a preserve, keeping the seventeenth-century life much as it had always been.

This is now our life, we realized as we walked back under the slowly darkening sky. The key and entry gate to the Moulin were becoming familiar.

We were home.

11

Sanglier

One of the things I did not know about Elizabeth before we got married was that she is an inveterate collector. She had a gorgeous small house in the "M Streets" neighborhood of Dallas, known for arts and crafts bungalows. It was full of French antiques and classy art on the walls and stylish furniture. Very tidy. The kitchen was well stocked. The linens and flatware chic.

That looks promising, I thought.

One day I opened a bedroom door and was surprised to see a different sort of décor and style. A room filled to the brim with old copies of *The New York Times* and *The Wall Street Journal*, books stacked to the ceiling, piles of papers and ledgers and files strewn in between piles of other piles. In the distance I could make out what looked like a window.

Tentatively I asked, what are you going to do with four-year-old copies of *The New York Times*? (I had peaked at one of the dates.) As if I had posed an idiotic question, she answered, there may be things in there I want to read again. Seeing that some of the papers had never been read, I decided to let it go and beat a safe retreat. Maybe it was just a one-bedroom addiction.

In France there are various levels of stores dealing in secondhand affairs. First, you have the *vide grenier*—literally, "empty the attic." Think of "car boot sale" if you are English. Rummage sale, in other over-stocked countries in the world.

Next level up—not sure about "up," but you get the point—is the *brocante*. Your French dictionary offers, "bric-a-brac trade." That sounds right. A slightly tarted-up version of *vide grenier*. Less, well, junky. (Don't tell her I said that.) At least the things are dry and organized into categories. You will find used books, kitchenware, art of various description, furniture, electronic equipment now out of vogue, and pretty much anything in the bric-a-brac genre. Germans will have used chainsaw blades, underwear, a fan belt collection, and electronic equipment in vogue but broken or missing a part. You can probably pick up a push reel-mower, with rusty blades. The French are not that tacky.

Next up is the *dépôt vente.* In some ways this is just a very successful *brocante*, a kind of industrial grade version of that genre. There was a very nice one in Aix-en-Provence, though the last time I was there it had moved to a village ten miles away. A sign on the door gave you directions, or what bus to take. I guess they had outgrown their warehouse space, or were driven out of town due to its now more chic, *haute de gamme* character. I confess I liked that store. Some very nice "brown furniture" could be found. Armoires and nice dining room sets. Books. Art.

As an aside, I had lived in St. Andrews, Scotland and had need to fill up bedrooms for making money during The Open Championship. The Scots are so clever when it comes to money. How was copper wire invented? Two Aberdonians fighting over a penny. They had a super Scottish version of the *depot vente.* Not wanting such good stuff laying around too long, each Friday morning they had an auction. On the Thursday before, you could pop by to see what kind of goods you might want to bid on. One day upon leaving the auction store in my car, I turned and happened down the street behind it. What was the store further down that street? A funeral parlor. Those clever Scots. In one side and out the other.

Finally, you have *antiquités.* Now we have moved up a notch or two. A famous suburb just above the *périphérique* in Paris is an entire rabbit-warren of *antiquités*, and all the various genre above thrown in for good measure. Even to mention the place and Elizabeth would start to get excited. You antique lovers know it. Think Isle-sur-la-Sorgue in the Provence/Luberon area. French Affaires hosted trips exclusively for people buying antiques. You could toss in for the ship container and share it with several others, fill it up, and still come out 50 percent ahead than if bought in the US. The place is awash with shoppers and clever shipping companies.

At least I was warned ahead of time, before we moved to France, that this was a passion of Elizabeth's. The darn establishments post their signs well in advance, not unlike "Pedro sez, 92 more miles," as you head down I-95 to the South of the Border Tacky Capital of the Universe.

If she were busy doing something and I spotted the sign first, I'd try to engage her in conversation. What kind of wine was it we had last night? Can you look in your handbag for some Kleenex. After you've been married for a while, this is like a blinking warning light, "Brocante ahead, Chris is asking dumb questions." Finally, I just gave up and decided to make the best of it. I might just find a nice knick-knack I could buy and re-sell at the next *vide grenier* shop.

We were in the Medoc during the summer I mentioned above, and the place was filled with these shops, especially in the northern part. Elizabeth would find flyers in the supermarket or on sign boards. I had been invited to play golf with some church people, and I was able to beg off. You go girl. Knock yourself out.

Now having lived in Scotland I was well accustomed to driving on the left (wrong) side of the road, seated right and shifting with my left hand. So, I felt a bit anxious as Elizabeth got behind the wheel and secured her seat belt. To drive on the right side of the road, in a car whose steering wheel is on the right, shifting with your left hand, in the Medoc full of traffic circles and tight roads—I knew that she was the champion of the 24/7 *brocante* marathon, but I was worried all the same. Are you going to be OK? She looked at me with something like scorn. Go play golf. I'll see you in four hours. And off she went. So much for a husband's kindly concern.

And sure enough she was there when we came off the eighteenth green. She shared a drink with our friends from church before we headed out. The good disposition and breeziness meant she had hit the jackpot. I imagined the station wagon filled to the brim.

She hadn't done too bad a job and there were some nice purchases, I had to confess. I was beginning to get the disease myself, I suppose.

One nicely framed picture showed a typical Medoc scene from the early nineteenth century, before Napoleon III had dispatched Baron Haussmann. The Medoc, like the lands of Gascony to the south, had once been full of bogs. The land was used for grazing sheep and other small cattle. And those who tended for them wore wooden shoes and worked on stilts. Makes for a nice painting and a piece of memorabilia, I agreed, from our time there in the summer of 2010.

Haussmann brought the Dutch down to introduce sophisticated dike systems along the Gironde and at other key points. The water was drained and then managed, and acres and acres of pine trees planted. So now the Medoc has a delightfully sandy, wooded interior region, with high-end vineyards on the west bank of the Gironde.

One thing that remained from earlier days, or perhaps enhanced by the forestation, was the hog. In French, *sanglier*. When we took occupancy of our gite for the six-week stay, the owner (a man from church) warned us to be careful if out hiking.

Elizabeth is from Texas, where the hogs are prolific, Texas-style enormous, and injurious of all in their path. They are culled by men in helicopters. In South Carolina we have hogs as well, but Texans would likely laugh and call them piglets. Elizabeth and I smiled at the kindly host as if to say, hogs we know, thank you.

Well, sure enough, you could hear them snorting around at dawn and dusk. One morning we were out jogging and got cornered by momma—or we cornered her, with her babies—and had to beat a quick retreat.

All to say, we learned that the *sanglier*, like the *vide grenier*, *brocante*, *dépôt vent*, and *antiquités* are indigenous to France, and all over the country.

We were living now in the Forest of Fontainebleau and the *Trois Pignons*. The *sanglier* are thick on the ground, joined by its close friend the *chevreuil*, or roe deer. Makes sense.

The kings of France did not descend on Fontainebleau to hunt rabbits.

12

Soulac Dimanche

ALONG WITH THE OCCASIONAL hogs, we were struck by the many surprises that this region of France presents. Our assistant at the church in Soulac was a well-known personality in the Medoc, earning her the sobriquet "La Reine du Medoc." A single woman in her early seventies, effervescent, an infectious smile, she had worked for the Rothschild family in their international wine trade affairs. She lived in Pauillac on the Gironde, and her office had been at Chateau Margaux. She gave us a private tour. I learned that the premier cru often tasted better than the grand cru. The latter was for investors, who let it age and gain in value before it was opened.

She also lived, as it happened, on the Tour de France route that particular summer. She invited her local friends and people from the congregation in Bordeaux where she worshiped for a celebration of the famous event. I will never forget, Elizabeth and I on her balcony, watching the thunderous banging of the side rails below as the cyclists zoomed by. This would be the final "time trial" event before they whisked off to Paris for the finale.

And the Atlantic beaches. Anyone who has been to the more famous Riviera coast knows it is like a sardine tin, your beach blanket like a postage stamp in a booklet of stamps. If you can find one at all, or a parking spot not two miles away for that matter. I recall us going to what we thought would be a quiet beach spot west of Toulon, in August. Saint-Cyr-sur-Mer. About two hundred meters from the town center, it was clear this was a doomed mission. Traffic stalled, no parking places, people pulling their vehicles into improbably tiny slots not meant for parking. We just turned around and went home. The sandy beach and blue water beckoned, but we saw only masses of flesh, like the puppy pile at the breeding kennel.

If you want wide beaches, ample parking, great surf (if a bit rough; this is a surfer destination), great beach walking, long empty stretches, you have come to the right place. You typically park high above the sea below, scamper down nice trails, lugging your beach necessities, come to the bottom and survey a grand choice to call your own for the day. You may also choose between full nudity, if so inclined, or topless, keep your *maillot de bain* on, or some mixture of the last two.

Elizabeth and I were staying in Carcans, and so the closest beach was Carcans Plage. The area is not crowded, so we tried several spots, Lacanau, Hortin, Pin Sec, and others. Our favorite was Pin Sec. High above the beaches, you parked. There is a super seafood restaurant there, more like a stand, but with places to sit under beach umbrellas. Population, fifty beachgoers, ample parking. Take that Saint-Cyr-sur-Mer.

At this special spot, down on the beach, one sees unusual concrete installations. Like the huge tops of mushrooms, emerging from the sand, a hundred feet across. Now splotched with bright, happy, summer colors. Surf boards stacked alongside. Children playing inside their little cockpits. Dads throwing frisbees. Surf breaking. What a bucolic scene.

Since the allied invasions are associated with Normandy, one forgets that the Germans (who had commandeered the French population to build submarines in La Rochelle not far north, above the Medoc) thought the enemy would land here. The Atlantic Wall. We were looking at bunkers. Their resemblance to those at Pointe du Hoc now coming into frame. Not high on a cliff, however, but along the sea.

German bunkers become the playground for little French children fifty-years on. The joy of beachgoing replacing the fear of Nazi occupation, all within the lifetime of older citizens living in the area.

On Sundays, Elizabeth and I would drive north to Soulac-sur-Mer where I would offer church services in English. The whole area attracts campers and campgrounds are prevalent as you move north toward Soulac. The idea was to attract holidaymakers wanting to have Sunday church. Germans, Scandinavians, the Dutch, and the British. English is of course now the common language, replacing French in that role two hundred years ago.

The Queen of the Medoc would help set things up. We had light attendance the first Sunday. Undaunted, she put signs on her little Peugeot and would drive around the camping grounds with a bull horn. "Come to church in Soulac-sur-Mer. 11:30 a.m. At the Temple."

By "temple" is meant the Protestant place of worship, in this case, *l'église reformée*. Soulac is also home to a grand Basilica, Notre Dame au fin des Terres. The little church where we gathered could hold about a hundred people, tops. We had about forty the first Sunday. The regular French Protestant congregation met at 10:00 a.m. They had graciously allowed us to use their parish for our six-week-long mission.

The pastor was an attractive, intelligent-looking woman in her thirties. Basque. Jet black hair, setting off her starched white preaching-tabs overlaying her black cassock. The vesture of the *l'église reformée*. Her congregation was itself not sizeable. And decidedly older. Elizabeth and I went to church with them before our service to meet her and get a sense of the setting.

She spoke a bit of English, matching my bit of French at the time. Elizabeth was our go-between. We enjoyed each other's company, she was obviously intrigued to have this American and his French-speaking wife land on her doorstep in a remote corner of the Medoc. It was proposed that, alongside our intended arrangement, we would do an ecumenical service. Her usual congregation, together with our fledgling English-speaking, holiday-maker worshipers. We would split the difference and meet at 10:30. Flyers went out. The Queen of Medoc altered her bull-horn announcement accordingly.

When the Sunday arrived, there was a pleasant buzz in the air. People milling around prior to the service time. Strangers meeting. Smiles and awkward efforts to communicate. The French congregation was putting in an effort. They were proud and excited to have us descend on them.

A temple does not typically have a sanctuary as we may envision that. That is, a raised-up area at the front of the church, with an altar and lectern, where the clergy leadership conduct the service—a bit "set off" in some architecturally designated way. The congregational seating, rather, extends right up to the front of the church. The reading/preaching lectern and sacred table are in close proximity to the front row of seating.

When the congregation is filling up a third of the space, the effect is different than when the church is full, as it was, happily, on this occasion. The ten of so front-row seats were grabbed by the first proud French worshipers. They had hustled up for a front-row view. This is our church! Their pastor is to host an American who has come to Soulac and has brought fresh faces to worship with them. The church was full. French, Dutch, Scandinavian, British, and German. Perhaps others as well.

Mme Pasteur and I had discussed the format. The service would be in French. I was to preach and she to lead the worship as her people were accustomed to. Others would follow as able. I can recall being seated beside her, curious faces looking at me from about five feet away. I would preach in English, so everyone could be a tad equally discomfited.

I asked my wife if she would offer a translation in French. She looked at me as if I were asking her to detail the car or do the taxes. Come on, girl, they will love it. Reluctantly—you owe me one—she agreed. I gave her my text before the day so she could familiarize herself with her role as *traductrice*. I still owed her one.

Mme Pasteur showed me the *feuille* or one-page printed service sheet. This was not a high budget operation. They also had hymn books in the thirty or so now full rows of seats. The sign board up front indicated the hymn numbers. I do this sort of thing regularly enough, I thought, to take a look at what she had chosen. How charming. The final hymn would be one that had verses in different languages. How ecumenical. Great idea.

10:30 came, a simple bell was rung, and off we went. I judged the morning as going very well. It came time for my address. I could tell from the faces staring up at me that some were listening clearly and others hadn't a clue. The French congregation was predominantly older, and resolutely middle or working class. They didn't have CNN on their TV sets. English is not spoken. I had figured as much so wrapped things up with a flourish of some kind when the short homily ended.

Now it was Elizabeth's turn. Being now myself a spectator, I could see the before and after shot. Every French head was turned to her and listening to every word. Nodding, smiling, oh, yes, of course. Well done. Thank you. Their faces glowed with pride. Our language, thank you very much. You are so very welcome here. *Bienvenue, tout le monde!*

I wanted to elbow her and say, now you owe me one. But she took her seat in the front row with the others. Soon the service would draw to a close. I was very pleased. Mme Pasteur was very pleased. The congregation was very pleased. The holidaymakers very pleased.

She rose and called out the final hymn. All stood and we started in.

First verse was in French. The lovely language echoed to the walls and ceiling above. Next, English. They tried and we did our proud and strong singing. Next Dutch. The *Néerlandais* were thrilled to be given a chance, and we faked it.

I am a fluent German speaker and so was glad to show off for the fourth and final verse. I started in with gusto. You could have heard a pin drop. The French people in row # 1 folded their arms across their chests. I modulated my tone and then joined the silence.

The bunkers on the beach had not fled from their consciousness. The days of occupation recalled. We were in church, a place of forgiveness and new life. Silence always precedes that, when there has been a severe wounding. Something felt right about the way the silence descended. A tribute to lost friends and family.

Generations come and generations go. Playing on the beach alongside those dreadful installations has its proper place now. God holds the times in his hand. Silence at the temple in Soulac-sur-Mer as well as children playing loudly on the beach.

When the service was over, I must add, what a grand celebration followed. What a rousing success our little ecumenical experiment. There were drinks and snacks, and new friends made. Elizabeth was thronged by the locals. Mme Pasteur and I had a hug.

God was on site that special day.

13

Our New Home at 7 rue du Petit Paris, le Presbytère

THE WORK ON OUR new house moved along steadily. No Peter Mayle anecdotes to share about sloppy or cigarette-smoking laborers, plumbers, joiners, roofers, tile men in the Luberon village of Ménerbes. We had a superb Polish team of four and we just let them get at it. This is also the beauty of being a *locataire* (renter). The work is under the supervision of Patrick, on behalf of the chateau of Courances. It is their property, and they want it done right.

We had one request. Knock out one wall space in the kitchen accommodating a small breakfast nook. We want the whole kitchen area. I agreed to plump for a gas oven/range that suited our cooking pleasures. The rest was up to them.

The Presbytère consisted of an entrance hall with toilet room under the stairs to the left, heading up to the first floor (US second floor). Beautiful, nicely worn, hexagonal, deep red floor tiles ran throughout the house (*tomettes* in French). Ones chipped too badly were replaced. They even ran up the stairs with an accompanying wooden tread and black wrought-iron railing.

To the right was the door into a large dining room, soon to be filled with antiques we would choose at a shop in Fontainebleau. A door led into the kitchen. From the window above the sink, you could see horses going by, clip-clopping along, rider's waist at eye level. Rue du Petit Paris, the lane separating us and the chateau grounds with a tall stone wall.

The main ground floor room was the lounge with grand fireplace. Two triple-glazed windows gave onto the stunning private garden area, that Elizabeth would restore. (In time, *Victoria* magazine would run a story on our house and her work.) Upstairs were two large bedrooms and two full baths. The "red room" faced onto the courtyard below, my office (to be), and the massive ramparts of the church. I loved to nap on the bed when we were fully moved in, as I could glimpse the cross atop the church from my window there.

The main bedroom faced onto the garden, with bath to the rear. On the top floor, *sous les toits*, under the roof, was a third bedroom and a vast storage room, unfinished. I say *sous les toits* because that is what is said, and because it is literally so. Looking up, one sees the wooden supporting strips in tidy rows, upon which are fastened the ceramic roof tiles, fully visible. It was a roof system proven to do the job, going back to the origins of the house in the seventeenth century.

Two features of the house I absolutely loved. It was not square. The houses on the streets in Courances, and all over France in villages like ours, are flush to the street on which they are found. In our case, coming to the house on the street, one would have no idea whatsoever what lay behind the nine-foot-high wooden entry gate, flanked on right by the house itself and to the left by the outbuilding and garage door. The house and street are exactly aligned. You could peek into our kitchen window, but it is high up and small. The house faces down on you on the street, the upper level retaining full privacy.

This means that the disposition of the house itself, inside the gate, is set up with an eye to the garden allotment behind it, and the enclosed walls and, in our case, the parish church. One senses this only a little bit when inside the house. But in the second bedroom upstairs, for example, the interior walls do not come together at ninety degrees, but, along the street and side, at something like eighty degrees. It gives you a sense of having been tucked into something larger and more determinative than the basic structure of the house itself.

And the second feature? The main bedroom we called the "blue room" and the second bedroom the "red room." The walls of both were covered in *toile suspendue*. On the spectrum running from mediaeval wall tapestries to modern paint covering, the intermediate phases are *toile suspendue* and *papier paint*, corresponding to the age and technical skill of the period in question. *Papier paint*, wallpaper. *Toile suspendue* is a strong, colorful fabric attached only at the points contacting the ceiling, floor and wall. You can, if you wish, tug it and see it is not fastened but is suspended (*suspendu*). This may also enhance the sense that the walls in red and blue rooms are not in fact square. Snug as a bug in a rug. Surrounded in the red room by period scenes, hunters, dogs, horses, and our friend M. Sanglier. In the blue, milkmaids, cows, streams, rolling fields. The cross on the church, our neighbor keeping watch over us.

In the basement, entered by separate door, is the cave. A grand stone vaulted space, always cool, its wine storage racks soon to be filled with crates of red, white, rosé—especially when the local Carrefour supermarket holds its biannual 50%-off sales.

I have mentioned the high water-table and abundance of water in the region. Beside my little office and lounge cottage, in the flagstone courtyard area, we had our own well. Not a bucket hanging from a rope on a wheel, to be dropped into dark waters below. Rather, a *source.* With a staircase of some twenty steps, leading down to the freezing water below. Almost below the church itself.

The neighbors spoke of *la Vierge* appearing there to a sick woman hauling up water. In the land of St. Blaise des Simples and St. Etienne the healer, why not? The massive ramparts of the church rise above the staircase in protective cover.

We will be given a key to the sacristy on the back left corner of our property, next to the high rear stone wall. From there one can make one's way into the cool, dark sanctuary, entering the world of a twelfth-century parish church and its worshipers, in Courances, our new home.

Cheminées - Carrelages
éléments d'architecture
01.64.22.05.46
06.84.61.30.14
06.85.54.21.81

14

Thierry May Antiquités

Meubles, éléments d'architecture

WE HAVE BEEN ENJOYING our time at the Moulin. Exploring the area. Getting to know neighbors in Courances and fellow *locataires* in Fleury. I am enjoying the hiking trails. We have now bought a car and done the many necessary chores for our new house. Utilities, healthcare, cable TV, and the familiar list goes on. We are enjoying life with our Catholic church friends in Milly.

I moved across the ocean to Scotland in the late 90s so have a rough idea of the drill. We were using the same company Elizabeth and French Affaires clients buying antiques in Isle-sur-la-Sorgue used for this move. They had agents in the US do our pickup in Dallas.

Predicting arrival times is a bit like predicting when fish will bite. They give you a ballpark date. Once your goods are in their hands, you are captive to their timetables. You are one, forty-foot container on a ship with myriad ones like yours. They took our goods overland to Houston and the ship left from there. Once that has happened, then things are a bit easier to calculate. They even give you a GPS tracking link.

The ships coming to le Havre don't go just directly there. Coming from the west they go to the farthest channel port first (Rotterdam) and then zig-zag their way back east (Bremerhaven, Southampton, et al.). Le Havre is last.

We weren't sitting on our hands until that happened. I am married to the collector without peer. There are several nice *antiquités* places in Fontainebleau. I am even reasonably excited. This isn't buying nice things for which one does not have any obvious immediate need. We are buying things for our new house. We are doing something useful, practical, necessary.

I repeat that all the way down General Montgomery forest road from Courances to the shop of Thierry May in Fontainebleau. We judged that the best place to start. As it would turn out—thank my lucky stars—it had almost all the goodies we might want, and more. I can leave Elizabeth to the many other *vide grenier*, *brocante*, and kindred shop options in our area that the French love to make available.

This was a truly amazing store—a *dépôt vente*. Compared with some of the places Elizabeth had taken me to, indeed, had begged me to go, this store looked truly intriguing. The genre on the sign, *elements d'architecture*, had a nice beckoning ring to it.

We entered the shop off a side road in Fontainebleau. It was one of those places that has nowhere to park. All the logical outside parking spaces are instead filled with *éléments d'architecture*. We are talking monumental stone. Enormous fountains. Granite fireplace mantles (elegant wooden ones inside). Paving material from yesteryear. Metal grillwork. Garden and patio stone items.

You weave your way through this labyrinth of impressive items mixed in with junk; sorry, the word is precise. We weren't in the market for things like this, not immediately at any rate. Or I wasn't. I could see Elizabeth going into calculating and mental note-taking mode. I headed inside as fast as I could, thinking that might move things along. Maybe a bit.

M. May was wandering casually about, having learned that the best salesman in shops like his pretend they don't own it or work there. They hum and act as if engaged in something serious in a corner of the room. Pricing a nice set of carving knives. Adjusting the arm on a huge stuffed bear. Repairing an epaulet on a "looks like a bargain" uniform from the war of 1870. Let your imagination go.

In fact, this is one of the nicer shops I have had the pleasure to visit. On my own steam, I might add. Very nice furniture. Lots of occasional tables in very good shape. Bookcases. Dining tables and chairs. I'd say we hit the jackpot, in fact. If we thought we'd about made up our mind, he'd open the door to a further room. I was so personally excited I even bought something that made no sense. I forget what it was, but I know that was the mood I had been in.

One very impressive piece was sitting right near the door. It and two others formed a set that would work very fine in our dining room. It was probably near the door because very big men said they would carry it no further. It was a massive seventeenth-century cabinet, taller than me, as wide as tall, with two doors opening on the top half, and two on the smaller lower half. Its compelling feature was its fine, cloth-lined interior, back of opening doors, back and sides and all the shelves. I'd never seen anything like it. It was full from top to bottom with blue delft plates, soup bowls, and attendant gravy boats and such like.

The other two pieces were lowboys in the same style. One could go in the entrance hall and the other could sit across the dining table with its massive counterpart. These rooms were not too far into our house, so no one would expire setting them in place.

Taking Elizabeth aside I said, he is having trouble selling this. It is impressive as a historical piece as one enters the shop, and while it has not been here since the seventeenth century, this is a piece more to admire than to move into your home. Our house, on the other hand, is its same age and it was made for our dining room. I'll handle this.

I gave him a price within 25 percent of his asking price and requested he throw in the delft. This would give us some wiggle room, as he could determine the value of the delft and decide whether it was going to be hard to get rid of as well. Elizabeth took over from here out. She is prettier than me.

He could probably see we were going to buy a good deal more, and so he agreed. Behind the scenes he may have breathed a big sigh of relief. But the three seventeenth-century pieces suited our new home perfectly, as did the half dozen occasional tables we bought. When you buy that much, you also get the delivery thrown in.

The work on the house was done. There was a bed on the second floor. The utilities were working. We would have enough furniture to work with. There was something romantic about letting its shiny new self just speak for itself, only 20 percent filled with furniture. Patrick sold us a nice dining table with ten chairs that Elizabeth would have reupholstered. Two armoires for red and blue bedrooms. The chimney was cleaned. We had an old settee the house left us. The kitchen was about done.

Friends from Dallas came down from Paris to visit us and see our new home. I have a photo of us all sharing a glass of champagne, bare walls behind us, in the large sitting room. The walls were timber and plaster, a kind of *colombage* effect but inside the house. A nice deep red setting off the timber framing.

And guess what? It was getting time to get our puppy. This would be his new home too.

15

Born in the Year of "M"

Wine-colored and taupe collar puppies have now had their shots. Arlette and Elizabeth have had several phone conversations—her accent challenges me but Elizabeth is the queen of French. We are leaning toward wine-colored. He has a strong head. A big strong saddle of black on his left side. Mme Salignac thinks his temperament is a bit calmer than M. Taupe. Fine.

We have agreed that she will bring our puppy up to Montauban, above Toulouse, to shorten our journey a bit and keep "operation escargot" memories in the mental rear-view mirror. We get our nice station wagon ready for our new companion. Elizabeth has studied things and, like a mom, wants to be sure he has everything a little boy should need for the journey.

As to the question of what we will call him, we have come and gone, back and forth. On reflection, we have decided "M" is more challenging than other first letters for naming a dog.

There's General Montgomery, associated with the region. He used the chateau of Courances as his HQ after the war. NATO was first headquartered in Fontainebleau. (I did not know that until we moved there.) He had built a road to expedite his comings and goings through the forest that was now our road as well. But naming a French dog after an English field general? No. Besides, "Monty" sounded all wrong as a nickname.

What about Marquis? That suited our chateau context. No, too pretentious. (As it would turn out, taupe collar would be called by that name.)

Montbrun was the name of the *ruisseau* (stream) that gave the name to his breeding kennel. Arlette said, too confusing. Repetitive. Montbrun of Ruisseau Montbrun. OK, not Montbrun. I thought it had a strong resonance.

Our favorite author was responsible for our favorite books and films, the writer from Aubagne, above Marseille, Marcel Pagnol. *La Gloire de mon Père. Le Chateau de ma Mère. Jean de Florette. Manon des Sources.* The list goes on.

"Marcel" he would be!

It had a nice casual sense, French, not pretentious. A "Marcel" as it turns out, is the name given to the T-shirt worn by laborers, without sleeves. Just straps. We would learn that our puppy had the same kind of insouciant swagger.

We had yet to learn what kind of "Marcel" he would prove to be. And since he is standing in front of me now as I type, Marcel is, well, the dog before me. Stop typing, let's go for a run, his presence says.

There is a great scene in *My Father's Glory* (1957) by Marcel Pagnol, when the family are making their way into the hills above Marseille for a long summer stint. Mother and two squirming boys, like Marcel in his puppy pile, and a little girl newly born to her. The father is a schoolteacher. His sister-in-law married later in life a wealthy, Marseille-born, kindly man: Oncle Jules, as he is known, proud husband of Tante Rose.

They have taken the streetcar as far as it goes through the outskirts of Marseille. A man from the village where they are headed has been hired by Oncle Jules to pick them up and ferry them by mule and cart to their destination. He could easily be wearing a marcel. It suits him.

He's a bit classier. *Tricot*, sweater, no shirt.

As they lumber their way up the path, he points out the peaks in the near distance and proudly names their names in his heavy Provencal accent. He is at home in his hills. *C'est Tête-Rouge* (Red-Head), *c'est la Taoumé*. One also calls it *le Tubé*. He beams as he pronounces their names.

Ever the teacher and a bit out of place, the father asks, what do they mean and where do the names come from? Not entirely getting the question, he responds, the names mean what they are. *Taoumé* (also *Tubé*) is that prominence I am pointing to. With that, he smacks the mule's rump and off they go.

"Marcel" is that dog he will become in our life.

We have the same long road trip, a bit dull, but no serious traffic to contend with. Elizabeth and I have time to relive memories of our first married days in France. Our love, our adventure. "Le grand voyage," as Brel sang it. We feel our little family is forming in our new home in Courances, next to the church with strong walls and a cross to look down on us.

Elizabeth visited France three times in 2009, and we were married the day after her birthday, on the 19th of December. We wanted to visit a region neither of us knew. We chose the Dorgogne, the region in southwest France named for the river flowing from east to west to the Gironde. It is a time of the year without tourists. We rented a car at the Bordeaux airport and drove to Bergerac. It was a few days before Christmas.

We had arranged to have a drink with the Anglican chaplain for the region (full of Brits with second homes there). Here it was that we decided on the summer mission in the Medoc. We wanted to be able to return and spend a longer stint. We finished our meeting and our drinks, and I went to get the car I had parked on the street.

Coming down a narrow street the tire rubbed the curb and blew out. Snow was falling. I prayed our *Lune du Miel* (honeymoon) would not become a nightmare (*cauchemar*). We were in rural France, Christmas was coming, would there even be a Hertz office in town and would it be open? I walked down to the café and told Elizabeth.

She phoned Hertz and it turned out—thank God—there was an agent in town. It was dark now. He came to meet us, looked at the tire and cursed his colleagues in Bordeaux. The tires were shot. We would have had a blow out on the way to our honeymoon spot, an hour and half away. The Chateau de la Treyne Elizabeth had picked out with its sumptuous décor and charming rooms. She had made a dinner reservation for 8 p.m.

The agent was a godsend. He had another, better car that he swapped out for us. No paperwork. Off you go.

The snow was falling more heavily, wipers keeping up with the pace. It was an SUV type vehicle and much more suited for the roads and our adventures to come. Everything was going to work out fine. An hour delay. Relief we both felt not to have had that accident outside of Bergerac, for we were soon in the Perigord Noir with nothing like the same population or services.

We share these recollections on our drive to pick up our puppy Marcel, on the A-20, passing the exit sign reading "Souillac," the town ten minutes north of Chateau de la Treyne where we turned that snowy night seven years ago to begin married life together. Then the sign for St. Cirq Lapopie, one of the "plus beaux villages de France." We would stop for the night there after picking up Marcel, only an hour away to the south.

Seven years. Where did the time go? What rich adventures that night heralded, that we would share husband and wife, companions on the grand voyage of life.

16

Bringing Marcel Home

SAINT-CIRQ-LAPOPIE IS A FAMOUS destination in a location we had come to know and love. In the Lot department, thirty miles east of Cahors. The village sits some three hundred feet straight above the river Lot and it was famous as a defense position in the Middle Ages. This is in part what makes it one of *les plus beaux villages de France.* We had never visited, as it is a bit outside the orbit of trips French Affaires takes to southwest France. The famous pilgrimage site of Rocamadour is a must for clients, and Saint-Cirq-Lapopie is another hour to the south.

Both Rocamadour and this pretty village where we spend the night are on the same chemin/camino headed to Santiago. St. Stephens Cathedral in Cahors is the next major stop, due west. Our purpose on this occasion is simply to have a quiet place to stroll and spend the night. Montauban is only an hour south by car, and that is where we are to meet Arlette. Our minds are on that. We found an excellent restaurant, *un des plus beaux restaurants* for the town carrying that same prestige.

We slept well in the quiet village and went down for *le petit dejeuner.* We are mindful of needing to meet Arlette and then make the entire return journey with our little charge the same day. Marcel will be making his first (of many) road trips in the little space we have set up for him in the rear of the station wagon. I have found a little crate that fits well. We want him to get use to that training routine from the get-go, so he feels it is his own house.

Arlette is waiting in her own station wagon at the rest area we have agreed. Our hearts race a bit. This is Elizabeth's first dog since childhood. I had a demanding Weimaraner I had to leave with my brother and sister-in-law when he was six years old, due to the quarantine headaches in the UK, when I moved to Scotland in 1998. So, the present routine was more familiar to me.

She brings us our new bundle of energy. Marcel! Exchanges like these are not unlike dropping the dog at the kennel for vacation. Make it quick. We get Marcel comfortable in his crate, get the paperwork from Arlette and promise to give her a call when home. Elizabeth stays with Marcel as I wrap things up. I ask Arlette if this is a hard thing for her. My memory is her responding, not really. She has done it many, many times. Off we go. *Allons-y.*

The little guy whimpers from time to time. But just as expected, he sleeps. We make regular stops so we can walk him and make sure he is doing his business and getting water. Elizabeth is *la bonne maman.* It should take us about five and a half hours. That's not too bad a journey time.

We make good time and arrive in the late afternoon. It is late April. I recall the saying, *en avril ne te decouvre pas d'un fil, mais en mais, fais ce qu'il te plaît.* Don't take a thread off in April, but in May wear what you want. The day was bright and spring-like warm. We park the VW in the customary spot across from our wooden gate. Out we bustle our little guy.

Our home set-up could not be more ideal for an eight-week-old puppy. Entirely enclosed. Three steps up from the courtyard to the garden and laid lawn. We have blocked off the stairway to the well. Safe as houses, as the British say. We let little Marcel find his way on his own and make himself at home. I have a video of him that Elizabeth made. I am rolling around on the grass next to Marcel doing the same. I am a bit tired of driving and emotionally tired I suspect.

On the video I can hear Elizabeth's voice. Marcel is rolling and rolling and rolling, especially on his back. Is he OK, she whispers?

It is grass. It may be entirely new to him, and, in a word, he is happy. We are too. *Bienvenue notre nouveau chiot, Marcel. Tu es chez toi.*

We introduce Marcel to his house. The doors opening onto the garden and into the sitting room give him easy access to the patio and garden. He can just clamber in and out. We have set up his cage in the living room. If he whines too much, I'll bring the cage to our bedroom for a season. He'll figure out how to handle the flight of stairs in time.

We feed him and sit down together to relax over a glass of wine. Having been recollecting our honeymoon and the southwest-France trips of French Affaires, as we were down in the area, I recall a funny episode.

We were in the Lot Department. Elizabeth had planned some typical on-the-ground type events typical of the region. Foie gras production (we won't do that again). Goat farm for chevre cheese (ditto, very stinky and nasty goats). Truffle hunting. Yes! We visited a famous site for learning how this is done.

Pigs have been largely replaced by dogs in the hunt for truffles. In the case of the truffle farm in the Lot, Labradors were to go-to breed. She told us all about how truffles grow, near what kind of tree, the rings they establish for good production, and so forth. We walked about her stand of trees followed by a trusty yellow lab.

What is the biggest challenge, be it with pig or dog? Why, how to stop them eating the prized truffles when they find them. They think they are yummy too.

She showed us the little wooden ball they soaked in truffle oil. You bury that, as if it were the valuable original being sought. The first time you let the dog hunt for them; here is where they start. They find the "truffle" in record time, dig it up, and chomp down. Ouch! This apparently keeps them from consuming the truffles when they find them or at least make them hesitant as the hand reaches in to grab the treasure from their mouth.

As she was explaining this to our group, I noticed that the famed truffle hunter yellow lab trailing us during her talk had an odd black spot on his rump. I'd never seen that marking on a lab before, as they are usually all black, yellow, or brown. What about that black mark, I asked?

She smiled and started to explain. Her famed truffle dog had such a reputation for quick work, someone kidnapped him. And they tinted the yellow lab black.

Fortunately, dogs in France are chipped and they recovered the faithful hound in no time. It had been about a year for her yellow coat to return. There was just this one black splotch left.

Marcel is a white dog with a riot of black spots all over his body, so it would be hard to call him a white dog with black spots or a black dog with white zones here and there. Neither. He's simply Marcel. Our dog. Sleep well tonight. It has been a day to remember.

17

Nos Biens Arrivent

OUR THINGS ARRIVE FROM the United States. I'd say, at last, but the world of moving is one where you'd best throw away your watch and your expectations. You'll just get angry. Movers have you. End of story.

Though just one thing. They tried to tie things up at the port of l'Havre. Paperwork. Customs. Things we wouldn't understand. That, of course, would entail surcharges for storage there.

I found a web address for none other than the person—it was in fact a woman—running affairs at the port. I thought, what the heck, I'll write to her and complain. Can't hurt. Probably won't hear anything.

Would you know, she wrote right back. Said she understood the situation. She would release whatever sticky-wickets the shippers claimed were hindering them from handing things over to the local movers to bring down from Normandy to our house. Consider it done.

It was a pleasure to forward the note to the crafty crook trying to take more money out of our pocket. The things would be on their way tomorrow.

Rarely is there such an efficient, rewarding, just settlement of what should always have gone that way. I cautioned myself that it was a once-in-a-lifetime situation and to just wait to see the vans rolling down our narrow lane. And by God they did. The next morning your French moving types arrived from Normandy, rang the bell, and started their work. We were moved in by day's end.

I recall that some of the alleged hold-up had to do with our car. The port HQ waived whatever the movers claimed was necessary and gave us instructions where to go to have the car checked out for safety issues and EU regulations. We had plenty of time. I think a month is what she said.

Just inside a month to get it all done. We had to get new tires, and they disconnected some light features on the front sides of the Mercedes sedan, and we were off. It was a cool experience since most of the cars they were checking out were in the 500K euro range. The customs control place was located at a former racetrack, with a banked oval course. The guys getting to go for a spin in those babies had a lot more fun than in our C-class sedan.

The last thing into the container in Dallas was the first thing out in France, our car. Complete with Texas plates. It was fun buzzing around our three-street village during those weeks watching heads turn. Now just who has moved into the Presbytère, strangers we had not yet met would wonder. I guess they really are from the US. Texas even. Will we see cowboy hats and boots? Isn't J. R. from Dallas? You don't recognize the name when the French pronounce these initials. Gee, Err. They smile. We wonder what they are saying.

We had made a good head start on furnishing the house already. Our US things completed the job. But with a second car, Elizabeth would be off to find all the closest *brocantes*. If you have a great storage space *sous les toit*, it just insists on becoming its own *dépôt vente*. Fill it up and then pick out what you need as time allows. No hurry. Everyone a winner.

Marcel watched all this with what was quickly revealing itself as his ironic wisdom. I'll sit out back in the yard and just bug the workers when it looks like things are moving along too efficiently. Aren't I cute. A puppy. I think we put the crate outside and locked him in. He could follow the action as men went in and out of our big wooden entry gate, both doors now blocked open.

When the work was over, we gave them a tip—they weren't in on the port scheming—and off they went, ready for another job tomorrow.

We had been living in France for some months now, and our house was coming into form. And Marcel had joined our adventure.

The *élevage* where he came from, as with its competitors it should be said, was a very classy place for this breed of dog. Ruisseau Montbrun had produced many champions in field and in show. I had "finished" my Weimaraner with a professional show person when I lived in Connecticut. That time-consuming venture interested neither of us. Marcel was a field dog.

There was a club, *les Amateurs des Braques d'Auvergne*, and joining that was something that interested us and so we did. France is not large. The field trials looked like fun. Another excuse to "do some research" on new and often lesser-known regions, as well as meet interesting people and a slice of culture owning a dog like Marcel would open us onto. *Les amateurs* kept up with all the new dogs coming onto the scene. It was not a big family. It was a close and personal one. We would make lots of friends during our time in France attending field events.

Marcel's brother Marquis would become the top show dog and eventually #1 Braque in the World. I confess a bit of relief that we had not picked him. Owning a dog of that quality is something like a full-time job. Serious business. Showing all over the continent and then the breeding menagerie.

We now lived in ideal field and hunting territory, indeed, a much sought-after region for that in France. On daily walks with Marcel, on the chateau grounds and on the forest trails that surrounded us, I could see his natural aptitude. He would raise his right paw, point and hold by God's gift in his genes. He would just need some refinement before, when he was fully grown, he could go on a hunt. The field trials were the best way to check his aptitude, and to see his conduct around other dogs.

We looked at the schedule and where the events took place. Soon we would be joining in. For now, he was free to point pheasants in the woods, and scamper after them. He was growing up. Doing what he was bred to do, doing what came naturally to him.

18

La langue française and la vie à Courances

We are now moved in. Marcel is loving his new home and surroundings. Every morning, we rise, and after a coffee, he and I head to the chateau park. We have a big ancient key to the special entry door just down the lane. One of the perks of being a *locataire* is access to the grounds. Most of the renters live in Fleury so Marcel and I pretty much have it to ourselves. There is another couple who have horses who live inside the grounds, and we see them from time to time. The owners (the Marquise and her adult children) are rarely in residence, chiefly on holidays. They live in London, Geneva, and other places, due to taxes.

We get to know the various workmen and grounds crew.

I realize I need to up my French language game. Getting a haircut and making small talk is a real challenge. "Kids OK? How was the holiday? Did you try the new restaurant?" Elizabeth says, just stay silent. I am too extraverted. I'd love to ask Madame *Coiffeuse* what I sounded like when I first arrived and tried to find the words for "tapered, no line across the neck, can use clippers and scissors." She commented in our fourth year one time, smiling as we had gotten to know each other by then, *Vous étiez nul.* You were zero.

I can laugh now, and the language for hair salon chatter is its own genre, but I wanted to move up from A1 (basic). We were now living in France. All the interchanges—pharmacy, wine shop, supermarket, physician, dentist, government this and that, post office, not to mention our new friends at church and in the neighborhood—were in French.

I thought to check with the town council in Milly-la-Foret, and sure enough, they had volunteers who were ready to help *les etrangères* tackle the language of their new home. I was given a name and address. Off I went excited at this opportunity—it was also free of charge—to work on conversational French. I had also been paying for weekly lessons in Fontainebleau, but I needed to ramp things up.

I knocked on the door of 5 *rue de la république* and I was obviously in the wrong place. Pardon, Madame. *Je me suis trompé.* A very useful phrase when you are new in town. Back home, I phoned the volunteer. (Talking on the phone can be a special challenge.) It was the *rue de la république* in our own small village of Courances! How convenient. Five minutes by foot.

And so would begin the start of a long and treasured friendship. My teacher lived next to the boulangerie on the main street of our three-street-wide village. As with houses in the historical Courances, his faced the street exactly like our own. All you see as you walk down to the boulangerie are houses on either side of the street, whose actual property and disposition, behind the gate, you could only guess at. Or, if so inclined, use Google earth.

In his case, answering the bell, he smiled and welcomed me into his property. He must have had a good two acres. You would never in the world know that or guess it staring at his wooden gate, not unlike our own. You enter a kind of world-unto-its-own. Big swimming pool. Play area for his grandkids. A second residence to attract their parents, his grown children. All enclosed by a high stone fence typical of the village, including our home.

We would meet once a week. He was not a language teacher but had been a successful businessman (book printing) in Tours and Paris. He was retired to Courances. He would buy a small *pied à terre* in the sixth in Paris, at my urging. He and his wife were divorced and the social scene in Paris would be more conductive to female companionship than our otherwise very special area.

He had grown up in a big Catholic family, the son of the town physician whose office was on the ground floor of their big home in the Savoie. Since all we did was French conversation—his English was good enough to be able to step in when needed—this would become a very good way to get to know someone. Their childhood, work, family, hobbies, loves. And of course, mine as well.

He was an integral part of the village family. Also of Milly-la-Fôret and our other villages nearby. I should say a word about that.

When the Angelus rang at our house, you could hear in the near distance two other Angelus bells pealing. Depending on how the wind was blowing it would be the parish churches in Dannemois, Moigny-sur-École, or maybe even Videlles. In the Catholic Diocese of Essonne, there were many rural parishes in small villages like ours and the ones I just named. Obviously, at one point in time when the great majority of villagers attended Mass, each village needed a central parish church, and so it was. The church was a center of activity, usually next to the Marie or close by, and the most valuable bit of patrimony and history (*patrimoine*) proudly on display.

In the first years of the twentieth century, the law of laïcization was passed in France, separating the church from the state, and probably more significantly, the church from the schools and the educational role it had exercised down the centuries. Much of this history was relayed to me by Gilles, as he had been raised Catholic and knew and respected the role I had as Anglican chaplain in Fontainebleau. He would comment on how very religious people in the US were; they put their hand on the Bible to swear an oath! I said that was pretty much a habit of culture without any sacred significance, and we didn't have forty feet high crucifixes greeting you as you entered the town.

The separation of church and state had the happy (probably unforeseen) advantage for the church that the buildings would come under the care of the communes where they were found, and where they represented the heart of the villages and of the *patrimoine* so valued by the French. I am sure there are some communist-leaning villages in the south of France that don't let that get in the way of their strong anti-religious instincts, or even proper care for the buildings themselves. But anyone travelling through France knows how omnipresent village churches are, in a very good state of maintenance. A new roof? Of course. I want my funeral there. My daughter's marriage (after getting legally married at the Marie), and so forth.

This isn't Scotland where churches become pubs or private residences. Unheard of!

The parish church of Courances was part of the *secteur pastoral* consisting, in our case, of more than twenty parish churches and congregations. The distances were not great and that allowed for a big number being under the single care of the lead Curé. Hearing two or three ringing Angelus gives you the visual and auditory picture.

Of course, the combination of a clergy shortage and light attendance in our present day would give way to this manner of proceeding. The three largest congregations would have Mass each Sunday at 11:00. As for the others, the clergy (three when we came, two when we left) operated on a rota. All the parish churches had lovely sanctuaries and had been well take care of. So, they would be used for an earlier 9:30 service, and then the pastor would jump in the car and race to the 11:00 every-Sunday service. Vested, behind the wheel, knowing the roads well, he made for an unusual sight—except that the clergy were well-known and this routine familiar.

Each parish church had a deacon who was the *locum tenens* (local cleric) and who made sure everything was all set when the priest arrived at 9:30 and 11:00. As a clergyman myself, from an Anglican background that likes to talk about lay involvement (the people of the parish playing a role), I was impressed with how efficiently things worked, and especially how much responsibility for the parish life was in their hands. Music, catechism classes, school visits, even hospital chaplaincy. Sometimes a negative (fewer clergy) can become a positive. The laity are proud of their churches. Clergy, they come and go.

So, in the case of the parish church of Courances, next to our house, we would have Mass about once every seven Sundays at 9:30. Otherwise, we went to the 11:00, in our case at the church in Milly-la-Fôret, along with all the other faithful (*les fidèles*) in our village.

This is all prelude to saying that, in terms of general village life, our "family" extended to all those in the villages nearby who worshiped at Milly. Those who did not go to Mass (Gilles, for example) nevertheless belonged to this wider sense of family and friends.

I write this now so grateful that Elizabeth and I, and Marcel, were a part of this family. Indeed, our priest friend, Père Paul Mercier, would often ask me, when we had 9:30 Mass in our church in Courances, if Marcel was in the garden. If he were to prop open the sacristy door, his Auvergne Highness would march right in and nuzzle everyone in the pews.

I'd keep it shut.

As charming as that might sound, take it from me, Marcel upstages every event where you imagine yourself in charge. Yes, he's there, Père Mercier, better not prop the door open this day.

19

Tayac-les-Eyzies

One of the beautiful things about living in Courances is that Elizabeth has the most spectacular backdrop for French Affaires, LLC imaginable. Also, a real plus is no transatlantic flights from Dallas to Paris and back. So, she is in high cotton. Business is thriving. Our home is guest central. With the Pierres d'Histoire lodgings literally across the street, the sky is the limit. She reaches for it, doing just exactly what she has been wanting to do all her life.

My church work is light by stated contract and shared agreement. We live in a different location (and that by design), twenty minutes from Saint Luke's Fontainebleau (we meet on Sundays at the Catholic chapel at a school on the outskirts of town). I have my writing projects and PhD students to take care of. In time, Zoom will be the mode of delivery, seminars conducted from the mezzanine office in our outbuilding, now done over to a nice state. Complete with a spiral staircase—I didn't like it at first—whose asset is that Marcel can't take over seminars. He nestles in next to the wood furnace on the *rez de chaussée*, making odd dog contributions to the seminar from below me.

I continue to work on the French language, with Gilles, and my teacher Catherine in Fontainebleau. I would like something yet more intensive. I research language schools online. With French Affaires clients, I had done a couple one- and two-week stints in Aix-en-Provence. Three hours each morning.

Pre-COVID, there were quite a few residential languages school humming along across France. A very highly regarded one in Moustiers-Sainte-Marie in the hills above Aix has been recommended. This is the home of *faience* (Elizabeth has several pieces from here) and the famed Gorge de Verdon, with a gorgeous deep blue lake. The school occupies a former monastery, and the promotional materials look grand. I will visit it many years later, though after COVID it had closed as a language school. Lots of weekend retreats, yoga classes, and so forth have replaced this once august language school.

In my time in Courances, I did a veritable "Tour de France" of language schools. The famed accent-free Tours. Two schools in Paris. Elizabeth and I spent a nice week in the Gard, renting a cottage in the village where André Gide grew up, and I went daily for individual lessons in the center of the excellent town of Uzès. February can be cold in France. It was. Marcel liked it all the same. Roaring fires.

A residential school in Roanne, west of Lyon, specializes in language and culinary matters. The three-star *Trois Gros* restaurant was located there until recently, a cultural landmark for holiday travelers of old, going down National 7, before the dawn of autoroutes. Gilles would regale me with stories of his family loading up the biggest Citroën station wagon made, luggage piled high on top, bombing down the speed-camera-free highway en route to Brittany from the Savoie for the August holiday month. The other feature of this language school was that all the help—cleaning staff, cooks, administrators—were also required to speak French with us. True immersion, that.

One thing I would learn after overdoing the intensive modality one too many times is: You can't drink from a firehose.

A nice school in Sancerre below us focused on Loire Valley wine. It was in the middle of a vineyard. But I wouldn't choose to return to the school in accent-free Tours. It has a funky university feel about it, at least where I stayed in a rented apartment, and the main street I walked to school was full of unleashed dogs. (It was the capital of dog poop.) I am sure there are fine areas of Tours, and indeed I visited them, but that French accent on the streets has never caught on with me.

One of the most memorable schools I attended in France was in Tayac-les-Eyzies. You will likely recognize the name Eyzies as the famed center for prehistoric caves in this part of the Perigord region. Lascaux to the north is not visitable but a very fine facsimile cave has been mocked up to give you a sense of the colorful cave art that over time, and due to the exhaling of so many visitors, tends to fade. There are of course many other caves to visit, some of the smaller ones truly enchanting.

Elizabeth and I love the entire region, of course, and French Affaires trips go there often.

The "school" in Tayac is in fact the atelier of a single French teacher, who after a lifetime of teaching big classes, all over the world (her husband is from Australia), decided to do just the kind of teaching that suited her. She and her husband bought a house in Tayac, a village a bit smaller than Courances and more mediaeval in feel, with some smaller gite residences alongside for language guests. They have a nice pool. The idea is to live there, with her and her husband next door, and the nice classroom space within the same footprint.

Elizabeth and I know the area well and opted to take a week at our favorite hotel in Tremolat, *le Vieux Logis.* Estelle, the owner, is a close friend. They have, in addition to the rooms in her *Relais et Chateau* manor, some ground floor gites ringing the lovely green space behind the main building. The same high standard. And better for Marcel, now our constant traveling companion.

Marcel is a bird dog, and he will chase absolutely anything moving in the air. Butterflies captivate him, as their flight is so unpredictable. If he loses sight of them—though his nose predominates, his eyes are very good—he will switch to chasing their shadows on the ground until he gets his bearings and then will resume chasing the real deal. Bees, flies, absolutely anything. I can see him racing around the green space, zig zagging with absolute precision, occasionally prancing with his front feet to get his balance, or to show off. Crowds would gather to watch him do his magic, not knowing entirely what he was doing since his prey was so hard to sight.

My mother was near the end of her life in hospice care when we were there. It was time for her to join her husband of seventy-years' marriage. I would pray each morning and light a candle for her in the small parish church in Tayac, before heading up to the lane to my teacher. Though not *fidèle* herself, she took charge of opening the church each morning, restocking the candles, emptying the little metal coin receptor, and seeing to its tidy state.

We met for two to three hours each morning. My French had gotten fairly good at this juncture of our time in France. Tayac was one of the last schools I visited. We would pretty much just talk or watch videos in her studio and then discuss them.

At our first session she asked what I wanted to do. Getting a sense of my level of French, she ventured, would I like to meet the oldest man in the village? French on the ground, as it were. Not knowing if this was an effort to not teach—she was one of the most professional and strict teachers I had experienced—I said politely, no. Maybe on the final day. I just wanted to stay put in her atelier and work on French.

It was a great week. Elizabeth and I visited favorite restaurants in the Perigord. We also went up to the Gardens of Eyrignac to say hello to the owner, a big fan of Elizabeth. We hadn't seen him since we moved to Courances, his favorite chateau in France.

Our close friend, the accomplished photographer Eric Sander, and his wife Claire had moved down from Paris to the countryside north of Le Bugue (Claire had grown up in Perigueux), their children now grown. He was outfitting a photography studio. They would put in a pool. It seemed magical to me, though I knew from discussions with Eric he had worried about the adjustment. It looked like it was working out just fine. He is another big fan of Elizabeth. They have done several photography-themed trips together.

On Thursday of the week my mother passed away, in her late eighties. Elizabeth and I were eating lunch in the tiny village of Paunat. My brothers, there with her at the end, called and we thanked God that her health struggles had come to an end. Her passing was quiet and peaceful. She was now with Tom, her beloved husband, and the Lord Jesus.

The final day of class arrived. It had been a very good week. I enjoyed working with Chantal. She had invited the local students she had in the area for a special afternoon session, but otherwise it was just the two of us. Elizabeth would invite her to join clients when she was next in the area. A new friend.

As we were wrapping up, a horse clopped by the window where we were working, the rider's head even with her studio *à l'étage*. I asked if we could go out into the little lane to see him. It reminded me our own little lane and the kitchen window from which we would watch horses walk by. Of course, *allons-y*.

There was a little troop of ponies making their way down the lane, and when they passed, going to wherever they were going, an elderly man came into view, with a little dog at his feet, a cane in his free hand. He was just across from us. The lane had the typical stone walls with a line of capping stones. I looked at Chantal and it was clear that this was the man she had wondered if I'd like to meet.

I crossed the lane with her to say hello. She greeted him and said I was her student this week. He nodded back. He seemed to be a bit blind, but his hearing was good. I'd guess late eighties, the same age as my mom.

I introduced myself and explained why I was there. He seemed interested. You are the elder statesman of Tayac, Chantal says. Can you tell me a memory of growing up here? My French is getting better, I thought, after a week of conversation with my new friend. You always feel spry on the final day of class.

He leaned on his stick and said, Yes. You see that wall there, behind you? When I was a young boy, I lived on this same lane. The Nazi's had occupied the village. Their main headquarters was at Brive, north of here, where the main train station is . . .

I could follow his French without trouble.

One day they brought a group of Maquis (resistance fighters) here who had been ratted out and brought down from their hiding places in the hills. There, where you are standing, they placed them by the wall and the senior officer drew his pistol, walked down the line, and shot each one in the forehead. I remember it as yesterday. They fell each one to the ground. The officer turned to me and said, place their coats over their eyes.

The next day they put us on a train and took us to Brive. Maybe fifty citizens of our village, not much larger than that. We walked off the train onto the platform and in the town square about the same number as our group, all men, were hanging by their necks. They had been hung and left there for viewing.

You see that? one said. We don't want to do this. I warn you. We will do it. Resistance will only lead to this. Be warned.

We got back on the train and came home.

That is the memory from my growing up here.

There was nothing to say, of course. I shook his hand, thanked him, and walked away with Chantal.

I had learned more in those ten minutes than I had learned in all the language schools I attended in my time in France. That will be a memory I will never forget, and will hold until I reach his age—not that far off now.

To learn the French language is to learn France. Thank you, Chantal.

20

Marcel dans le Fôret

Our pal Marcel comes from one of the finest breeding kennels in France. His nose is bigger than any other organ in his body, I'd wager (knowing nothing about organs, of course). When we go into the forest near 7 rue du petit Paris, out the track road to the east, past the cemetery and the Fallen Airmen Tribute, and I let him go, the fire behind his boosters lights up. He can smell game from a hundred meters, from inside the car. He is gnawing at the station wagon gate. He hits his head on it as he explodes forth.

I have purchased a hunting shock collar for him. If you know about these, first the dog hears a beep, then he gets a vibration when you push the next button on the hand-held device, then he gets an electric shock. It's a genius system. I wish I could use it for PhD students. All kinds of applications come to mind.

You set the number three shock selection (the English euphemism is "a nick") with the dog looking at you. Sit still, Marcel. Levels one through five are useless. A dog has a lot of fur. I use it on myself and four is like touching the electric fence of growing up in the country. Number six and he seems to think of something other than his next meal. I set it at six.

The idea is, if six gets a reaction from a dog sitting in front of you, then when he gets the beep, and then the vibration, he has fair warning. We are doing something serious here. Dad is doing something that matters to him. OK, I get it.

Once the collar is put on, he enters the world of "I am hunting" and that is the whole point. That said, when he is seriously hunting, I mean really entering the world of "I am Marcel," a six is useless. You hold the device and start moving up the scale. At this point it is probably too late. He's gone in a blaze of flying dirt and sand.

Because, when you enter the forest track across from Courances, past the cemetery, we are in pheasant land. Not just the usual birds (imported from Nepal) or the ones that are indigenized in places like South Dakota in the US, but big lumbering, brooding birds used to walking about, eating the abundant grain that pheasants eat right by their nests, and then watching TV and napping in the afternoon.

The chateau, like shooting clubs in the same spirit all over the world, has introduced these birds so their guests can hunt them and believe they are up to something mediaeval and hard and exclusive. I want to be charitable. But pheasants who brood in the forests and watch TV in the afternoon actually don't fly very much. When you startle them on a walk, they "get up," fly about fifty meters, and come back down, hoping the commercials have passed and some fresh grain has been discovered during their tiny sojourn.

And then one day they find their life has been disturbed. Routines upset.

Marcel is now in the woods. This is his world. What are all these pheasants doing here? I shall have to find out. I can smell them from 7 rue du petit Paris.

Obviously, our new dog will have to test his skills against other Braque d'Auvergne dogs his age. Also, this is a good way to make new friends at the venues for this all over France. *Les Amateurs* post a list of upcoming field trials at their website. They call this the *test d'aptitude naturelle.*

We find an event in the Berry, south of us, the historical name of a region now consisting roughly of the Loiret to the north, Indre to the west, and Cher in the southeast corner—three of the 101 Departments or administrative districts created by Napoleon. Our drive is about ninety minutes to a small field in the Loiret.

A nice late spring adventure. You get a little guidance on the location at the website. Off we go, leaving just after 7. Marcel senses something fun is up. We come to the village where we are to find further guidance in the way of signage, and see the glass covered announcement board next to the Marie. Good. We are not lost. We have about a mile to go, and signs have been posted by the road "*TAN—Braque d'Auvergne événement*" and the date. We see the SUV's and various cars parked in a field, with a table set up for registering. And of course, the cousins of Marcel on leads, or in the open boot of SUV's restless or calm in their crates.

We are greeted by our owner cousins. Elizabeth handles the *bavardage* (chatter, chit-chat) after we introduce ourselves and register. *Les amateurs* are keen on their dogs, and they know about Marcel. The dogs come from the kennels scattered across France, and everyone knows Arlette and her dogs (usually more black markings). I see versions of the breed far whiter in base color, and with less black.

There is very little in the way of explanation by the judge for the day, as to how this will unfold. I didn't take that as unusual at the time. I had also done no research about it, because I assume you show up, give your dog to the judge or assistants, and off they go. Wrong assumption.

Because when I agree to let Marcel go first, I suddenly get the sinking feeling I am supposed to know what I am doing. I am not dressed to stomp through the *chaume* (stubble field). I look about and see I alone look like the stupid American, in shorts none the less. Well OK, let's go. Can't be that difficult.

I let Marcel off his lead. Game birds have been placed at key spots by the helpers for the day. It isn't a matter of tricking you as you don't know where they have placed them, though they do this before the field trial begins. The dogs know what's going on. But this owner doesn't know what's going on so I am trying to play more of an active role than is necessary, with a whistle and arm gestures. I am helicopter parenting a dog who would naturally range left and right, or learn that in short order, without so much coaching. Or so I would learn.

I'm not sure why I chose to go first. I'm naturally competitive I suppose. Or let's get this over and we can have another coffee and relax. After all, I thought I was just giving Marcel to someone else, and I'd stand and admire next to Elizabeth.

Another way to put this (since in time I will know how to work with Marcel in the next field trials) is, if you had waited and let others go first, you'd have a clear sense of the *déroulement* (process) just by observing. Feeling a bit humiliated, we leave the field and then see how it is done with the eight or so dogs next in line.

In fact, I will learn, I'm not the first person to launch into field trial space a bit rusty. I watch the others and see better and worse owners working their dogs. And, I also realize that Marcel is very talented, and full of promise. I think I was just caught off guard about the role I was surprised I had.

After the last dog finished, a kindly man offered to give me some training. And into the field we went. He could see that Marcel had a lot of *aptitude naturelle.* We would all see each other again at trials down the road and he wanted us to have a better experience.

This isn't the United States. You don't wrap up the trial—the reason you came—and go home. The reason you came is for the Full Monty. Trial, awards, vendors, socializing, and something on the order of a three-hour lunch. Ah, the French. We sit at long, rough tables, on benches, across from each other and down the line. Aperitifs. One starter. A second starter. Wine of course. A main dish. More wine. Side dishes. A variety of desserts. Coffee and/or a *marc* (regional brandy).

Gradually the day takes on a different hue. We are making friends. The dogs can play with each other or be tucked into the vehicles. It's time for us to play and jostle and tell stories and promise to see each other down the road.

Les amateurs de Braque d'Auvergne.

21

Le Field Trial

When you stop to think about it, much of life resembles a field trial. Entering fields that are strange and confusing, though bright with promise. Mistakes are made. Learning follows. My favorite French expression is *c'est en forgeant, on devient forgeron.* It is in blacksmithing that one becomes a blacksmith. The too-hot fire, the busted knuckle, the misshapen ax head.

Learning French is its own field trial. One forgets that this is how life begins, how our maternal language is acquired. We listen to mom, we offer our sounds back to her, we slowly develop the ability to communicate orally. Oddly enough, then we go to school and take a course in "English." Why do we do that? To learn that the language we are already using has vast range, rules for proper speaking and writing, and the learning will go on for the rest of our lives.

When it comes to learning another language, as an adult, well, now we are not children but have learned to read and see in our mind's eye how words are spelled. Funnily enough, this makes learning another language challenging. I teach French now, and you can sense which learners rely on seeing more than hearing, the latter group much more willing to try to become children again. But we all lie on a spectrum, and another language is learned as we shuttle between our adult and our child selves.

As we banter along at the table, people curious what we are doing in the Berry in a remote part of France, in a barn in a field, I shuttle between my adult self and my child's self. You learn by persistence, by being willing to make mistakes, through listening to French and becoming comfortable with confusion, 15 percent becoming 30 percent comprehension, taking what can be taken and patiently waiting for more understanding. The same with speaking.

And guess what? I get to draft behind the language skills of my beautiful wife. If I am wearying—a three-hour lunch with conversation taxes one—there she is, carrying on without obvious struggle. I can take a break, smile and nod, and rest for a moment.

We meet a lovely woman who lives in the Champagne region. She sees obvious talent in Marcel and asks if she can be of assistance? She could work the field with him next time. Or we could come to her and she could put me through the paces and acquaint me with how to work Marcel in the field. I am motivated to be more adept at this and also want to relax and enjoy the ride next time. I think she also wonders whether he'd be good in the show ring. She shows dogs professionally.

Back in Courances and our first field trial behind us, we contact her. The plan is to come to her house in the Champagne region northeast of Paris. That's not too far from us. It is an area of France I do not know. "Doing research"—the all-purpose excuse.

We go up for the day. Meet her at her modest house. The house of someone who shows dogs, trains dogs, loves dogs. A sort of dog house with adults living there too. She has a special field nearby. She teaches me how to leave Marcel alone, trusting his innate *aptitude naturelle*. When and how to signal him that he's ranged enough in one direction and it's time to reverse course. How to watch for his picking up scent and then encouraging him. She suggests when I go home to continue to work with him by getting some live birds. The chateau grounds will be perfect for this.

Of course, like everything with a dog, you are not training him, so much as he is training you. I buy a couple of quail in the neighboring village of Dannemois from a man who raises them, and off we go to the park. The little birds chirping away in the makeshift container he's given to me for transporting in the car. Once home, I get Marcel, the gate key, and off we go.

He's revved up just at the noise and smell of them. I tie him up at some distance, out of sight, as I prepare. I know about placing quail from hunting them in Texas. You take a small sack and gently swing them in it. It makes them dizzy and "calms" them so you can find a place to nest them. In low brush, their habitat in the wild.

OK, good. Let's see how Marcel does. He needs to associate what we are doing together with what we are going to do in a field trial. Chris is with me. Quail are part of the deal. This means we are doing something out-of-the-ordinary. I'm not just romping around in the park.

I've learned he doesn't need much help. No whistle. Just voice commands so he looks at me and sees me pointing right or left. That does it. Our trial is a success. He ranges, points, holds, and I then let him catch the live bird in his mouth and bring it to me. With a lot of dogs, that is a challenge. They don't want to give the prey up. Marcel has a "soft mouth" and hands him over. I break their neck—sorry—and back home we go. I clean the birds for a nice quail popper: quail stuffed with cream cheese and wrapped in bacon and then baked until golden brown.

The point of this preparation is to make me feel familiar with what is going on. Bird, terrain, Marcel, his movements and manner of scenting. We find a field trial number two. Another new area of France to explore.

The short story here is that Marcel is a big success. I am proud. Elizabeth and I enjoy the same *test d'aptitude naturelle* fellowship and fun. Marcel passes his field trial. I think the word has gotten around that I have a great dog and a new person has come to see him work.

This lunch is more relaxed, or I am, and so enjoy it more. The new man and some experienced Braque owners come to congratulate me and Elizabeth. They want Marcel to enter the "best under-threes in France" competition, to be held toward the end of summer in Cognac. In the Charente, about four hours by car from Courances.

I'll check my calendar, I say, but know we will make this happen. *On se tient au courant.* We'll stay in touch.

We drive back so happy and proud. Our dog has passed his field trial and more than that, he has been invited to compete with the best in France. Perhaps his brother Marquis will be there.

Marcel sleeps in his little "cabin," the station wagon. This is the France we came to enjoy.

22

L'Éte en France

Over the course of our marriage, prior to moving to France, we visited almost every region. For ourselves, or because Elizabeth was organizing trips for French Affaires. The one region we visited more than others was les Alpilles. It's where we first went after meeting for drinks in Dallas, then celebrating Palm Sunday in Maussane with olive branches for palms.

Living in France changes everything when it comes to travel. Want to go to Champagne for a day with the dog trainer, no problem. Loire Valley, just down the road. Beaune for date weekends, two-and-a-half hours in the car, on a fine autoroute (without any *operation escargot*) with an entrance ten minutes from our house. Paris for dinner. Why not? We had by this time found a super dog trainer in our area who could board Marcel. She became a close friend. Marcel has always been more happy when he has dogs to hang around with, and she could break up any male squabbles.

Now we could visit our favorites places in les Alpilles in a seven-hour drive. Sometimes the tunnel in Lyon could slow us down, but after that, it was clear sailing to Avignon and further south to the area around St-Remy-de-Provence where we liked to stay.

As well, Aix-en-Provence is but an hour or so away to the east. The Luberon above that, with its palette of *villages perchés*, each one delightfully different. Rousillon with its deep ochre colors. The slightly chic Gordes, next to the Abbey of Senanque, its lavender fields a riot of color from May to September. Ménerbes, recovering from the invasion of Peter Mayle and fans of his books. The charming Bonnieux just below it. Ansouis, a small gem with a nice *restaurant etoilé*, looking south toward

Puy-St-Reparade. Cucuron, Vaugines, Mirabeau, where Claude Berry set the scenes for the films of Marcel Pagnol.

Elizabeth had spent much time in Aix as a French student from Vanderbilt, a city sometimes referred to as Aix-en-Vacances, or Sex-en-Provence, because of its popularity and charm for foreign visitors. We would see it become more refined and tidied up over the years of our visiting. The language school there is the base for the popular "live like a local" offering, with daily immersion in the French language at the international school.

But we liked the Alpilles for plopping down for a couple of weeks. Reading, swimming, walking, eating well, the many morning *marché* in all the local villages. Maussanne, Fontvielle, Moriès, St-Remy, Tarascon, and of course Eygalières. We rented a small house at the top of the village one summer, and used it as a base of operations.

If you are ever in the area in early August, be sure not to miss the Fête de la St. Laurent. We caught it one year entirely by accident. They line the main streets of this small village of eighteen hundred inhabitants with big wooden barricades. We had parked our car, coming back from St-Remy, to head down to the market on the 10th of August. Something is going on. Big horse and animal lorries had taken over the main parking lot to the west of town. Cowboys (in French *les gardians*) were proudly strutting about.

It comes as a surprise to many that the Camarque region south of les Alpilles is home to French cowboys. This is a slightly exotic area, located within two main branches of the Rhone as it spills into the Mediterranean. Flamingos, pink sea salt, bulls, and *gitanes* (gypsies) who come for an annual homage to the Black Virgin. The bulls are bred for a specific kind of bullfighting. Not a Corrida, where the bulls are slowly worn down and then killed, but rather a rite-of-passage sport in an arena, where colored ribbons have been placed in the neck band of these enormous bruisers. The contestants are to leap up, grab a ribbon if they can, and then find a way not to get gored or killed. Vaulting out of the arena is the tried-and-true way. It is slightly like a carnival to watch as an outsider, but serious business when you climb into the ring.

For this festival, they let their prized bulls run the streets, chased or herded by *les gardians* on horseback. The compact streets are short track for running—they go to the top of town near our summer rental and back down again—and thundering hooves on paving stones makes for a dramatic forty-five minutes. They run the bulls back into the transport vehicles at the end of the course. Take a break. And do it again later in the day. Time for a *pichet* (pitcher) of rosé and a big salade niçoise. When fun things are happening, the French are not in a hurry. OK, a second *pichet*.

In addition to the many places to visit and enjoy, we also had a friend from Dallas who owned a nice modern home next to the towering Mont Ventoux. It is an hour north of les Alpilles and almost into the Department of the Drôme. She lived in Crillon-le-Brave. A widow, she had also bought two nice homes for her adult children and grandchildren.

Crillon, for reasons I don't think anyone knows, unless it's just a nice place, is full of former diplomats. We got the impression that one gets moved around a bit in this line of work, and after a while you get to know your fellow-diplomatic colleagues. Parties at Bonnie's and at their homes always made for great conversation. Mostly British, they had been posted all over the world. Their stories were exotic, dangerous, but always full of adventure. Elizabeth became a very close friend to one charming woman who was undergoing cancer treatment. We all went to spend the day together in Avignon and then Carpentras to the south. We were so sad to learn she had not made it. Such lovely children as well.

Two stories in particular. The market morning at the nearby Bédoin was a fixture and all the cohort of friends would never miss it. We'd sit at a favorite café and order coffee and people took turns going to get pastries at the boulangerie across the street. We just hung out there all morning, taking passes through the marché, buying some things—I got a nice Panama straw hat, Elizabeth some summer dresses—and returning for more conversation. We'd either pack up shortly before noon, or sometimes stay for lunch. When you have interesting people and great conversation, it is easy to be content with doing nothing.

One year when we visited, the annual transhumance was underway. This is the time when the sheep and goat herders move their flocks to new feeding grounds, as the seasons turn. This is the magic of France—be it horses and bulls running the streets, or the transhumance, or watching lavender wands (*fuseaux*) being made by hand without change or variant or machinery—the rhythms of the generations, unchanged and preserved, catching you up in their music. You are in the same streets as on the market day, now swarmed by animals as they pass by.

The other memory was of a concert to which we were invited by "Friends of Crillon-le-Brave." Held in a tiny, ancient chapel, a short walk down a trail. I always worry about these local events. What are we in for,

Elizabeth? Can we bail out if dull or amateurish? She looked at me with her usual look. We are going. Bonnie's our friend.

The chapel held no more than sixty-five. It was full. It was early evening. We were to be listening to a performance by an opera singer. It was just him and an accompanist. The theme was an operatic piece concerning Petrach's famous climbing of Mont Ventoux.

As one account summarizes: The Italian poet Petrarch wrote about his ascent of Mont Ventoux (in Provence; elevation 1912 meters) on April 26, 1336, in a well-known letter published as one of his *Epistolae familiares* (4.1). In this letter, written around 1350, Petrarch claimed to be the first person since antiquity to have climbed a mountain for the view. Although the historical accuracy of his account has been questioned by modern scholars, it is often cited in discussions of the new spirit of the Renaissance.

Our opera singer, standing not three feet in front of me, seated in the front row, gave a similar brief summary before starting. No one climbed a mountain for pleasure. Keepers of flocks and herds, yes, but that's what they do for their livelihood. Seeing the vast world below from the top of the enormous dormant volcano, the poet Petrarch sensed the shortness and fragility of life.

Many say he invented the term "Middle Ages." To know the "middle" of something you have to have a wider conception of history and time itself. The before. The to-come.

You have to have a perspective from above.

OK, this sounds promising. Off he starts. There is something about hearing a professionally trained opera singer in full voice in a chapel holding sixty-five people. The hair went up on the back of my neck. The words, in German, sought to capture Petrarch's combination of astonishment and melancholy.

Elizabeth, thank you for insisting we go.

It is important to have a sense of where we are in our own lives. Your close friend from Crillon gone in her forties. The ascent to heights which produces awe, and which also reminds us of the grandeur that belongs to God alone, who gives us the span of life we have from his hand.

23

Le Jardin chez nous

THE FEDEX TRUCK HAS rung the doorbell, and they are dropping off a dozen big, thin square boxes. *Table pliable* it says on the outside. Elizabeth is up to something. Her trips to the *brocante* have yielded lots of goodies, and I have noticed a great deal of—to be sure—very nice, heavy linen tablecloths, napkins, and general table accoutrement (weights for napkins, napkin rings, little metal devices to hold an *etiquette* (from which we get the more general idea; it's actually a small printed card bearing the name of who is to be seated).

Back in Dallas, Elizabeth started a French Affaires cookbook club. The twenty or so ladies, guided by Elizabeth, would choose a cookbook. In groups, they would choose which meals each subgroup would prepare, including starter, main dish, side dishes, cheese, dessert and wine. I recall our house being transformed into southwest France, for example, with the regional dishes for which it is known. Cassoulet, truffles, foie gras, pork, sausages, walnut cake, raspberry tarte, champagne and regional wines for each course. You get the picture. Armagnac, I left out (southwest France cognac). Not to be missed.

There's a store in the seventh where you can buy a bottle for your birthday, with year and date stamped on the front. Ryst Duperon, on rue du Bac.

Now that we are in France, it's time to have a French Affaires cookbook club event *chez nous*. I have memories of several of these in France, Elizabeth surrounded by her many friends, excited to show them our house and our new manner of life.

The lodgings of Pierres d'Histoire are also perfect for this. The various *maisonettes* can be connected via shared doors, thus turning the place into one big buzzing cooking event. Plenty of ovens and cooking areas (each unit has their own) as well as our own house just across the lane.

Depending on the size of the group, we would gather in our own dining room to enjoy the finished product (all the courses), which could accommodate fourteen all nicely squeezed together. Once with a Pierres d'Histoire group, she just spilled out in the Japanese garden and set up tables there. Two assistants from the village to bring dishes and fill glasses. What's not to like?

Now I get it. This was the thought behind the stack of cardboard boxes newly deposited in our courtyard. Each one contained a sturdy table, eight feet long when set up (*déplier*) and latched tight. You throw gorgeous heavy linens on top of them, with silver clamps to keep them in place. Linen napkins. Etiquette holders. Flowers. Silver place settings. The blue delft from Thierry May Antiquités. A designer from Paris to aid some extra flair.

Our garden area is transformed. Seating for as many as twenty-four, or more if desired. Tables set at angles, filling up the laid lawn space behind Elizabeth's transformed *potager*, full of Ravel ceramic pots with plants. Bells from the church. Marcel chasing bees. Music. Champagne.

It is September. The angle of the light is perfect—there is a reason painters came to our area and formed the Barbizon School—with the daytime temperatures in the low seventies and no humidity.

It is hard to overemphasize the enjoyment and pride this brought my wife. We were living in a magical quartier. Our house is now filled with nice furnishings, and the walls are bearing paintings and etchings and historical scenes that she has found on her brocante adventures. The chateau grounds are there for strolling.

There is a sort of "lottery" for larger groups than the Pierres d'Histoire lodgings can accommodate. The winners get to stay in the chateau itself, in a two-story wing set up for guests but able to be accessed for French Affaires clients due to Elizabeth's impeccable taste and attention and the trust she has earned with Patrick and the Marquise.

Friends from church and our village neighbors are invited for an *apéro* or glass of champagne. They try out their English or find one from our group wanting to speak French. The cookbook club concept also means that everyone involved is also a sort of host to the others, each in their turn. The starters prepared by subgroup one are brought out by the proud cooks in charge of this segment. Subgroup two is next, and so forth. They compare and applaud or say, next time more salt, or whatever. It isn't a competition. *Chaqu'un à son tour.* Everyone at their turn.

The house doors onto our garden are propped open. The northern latitude means fewer flying insects. There isn't a screen in the house. Because the masonry walls are so thick, you open the windows at night when the temperature drops. In the morning, you shut the big exterior wooden *volets* (shutters, French blue of course) and the cool is trapped throughout the day. In the evening, one can then open the doors for the cookbook club traffic, shuttling in and out of the kitchen, through the large sitting room, and into the garden decked with such beautifully decorated tables.

And of course, I am the proud husband and host. I know half of the guests, and get to know the other half. We have assistants helping, so I needn't fill glasses or bring in new dishes. I can leave my seat at the end of one of the tables, next to Elizabeth, and pass from table to table saying hello and greeting old friends, and introducing our French guests. Our neighbors. Our family.

Marcel makes his own rounds, of course. He is on strict orders not to expect any food, though of course people cheat and sneak him this or that. He takes commands in English and French. He is bilingually disobedient. He is part of our family and also of our village. He eventually settles in a corner of the garden he likes, in the shade. Thoughts of his field trial conquests keeping him company, his eyes heavy with contentment. Happy to see so much joy and abundance.

All that is left is for every carefully wrought portion of the feast to unfold and conclude. It is nice no one involved has to go any distance, or get behind the wheel of a car. We are in a village of two-hundred-and-fifty people. Their French home is across the street. Night has fallen. Stars are shining down. Quiet and cool descend.

It has been a very good day. Elizabeth's French dreams now all a reality. For her, and for all the many friends she has gathered.

Bonne nuit. À demain. We close the wooden gate to our home and find our bed.

A day full of friends, food, and rich blessings.

24

Les Buveurs d'Air

In the second field trial, I asked that Marcel go last. I was still a bit gun-shy after being first in the field at the Berry event. People wanted him to show his best stuff, as I mentioned, and so were happy to comply. We got to watch all the other dogs and their owners before it was our turn. I could also observe the folks in charge of putting out the birds, and how they went about their placement. A field trial isn't about hiding a bird from the owner in the field. He isn't hunting. The dog is.

Marcel did brilliantly and passed with high honors. One thing, however, I took note of. Going last meant that there was a lot of bird scent in the field and stray feathers. For Marcel, it was a field full of quail *émanation*. On occasion, he'd stop and point hard where there was no bird, but just a feather. The judge took full account of this. As did the others. This wasn't the first field trial where that was a challenge. What it did show was that Marcel had a hyper-scent. His *flaire* in French parlance.

The drive down to Cognac for the "best under-threes" event takes you past Orleans, Tours, and Poitiers. By air, we are not too far from Soulac-sur-Mer and the northern tip of the Medoc. This is the Charente region. I pass the big Hennessey buildings coming into town. Cognac is the home of cognac. I have booked a hotel on the outskirts of town which allows dogs.

I have made good time and have the rest of the afternoon free. I didn't want to feel pressured. Elizabeth is doing a French Affaires trip and I'm on my own with Marcel. We find some paths along the Charente river, and I give him some exercise. I have the map and directions for the event, and I want to know the distance and the route so I can relax in the morning. I let Marcel run around in the field where tomorrow the competition will be set up. It is the fall now.

Back in town I find a nice brasserie for dinner, Marcel at my feet. This is one of the nicest features of France. The way they make room for pets. Marcel knows the routine and cozies up next to my feet. I think of the café in Fontainebleau where Elizabeth and I said hello to our first Braque d'Auvergne. The roads and adventures Marcel has taken us down, and that he will share with us in the coming years.

The event the following day goes well. Marcel is the runner-up "best under-threes." He gets a nice trophy and a medal with tricolor ribbon to hang around his neck. The competitors are all contented with the results and I am pleased. I've gone from rags-to-riches. I get on the road after the usual festivities, anxious to be back at le Presbytère before too late. I haul his crate into the courtyard of our snug home. Marcel heads up to his bed. *Il a gagné le trophée.* I put it on the mantle so Elizabeth can see it upon her return, remove Marcel's medal, and head into my own bed for a good long sleep.

Well done, *mon chien. Je suis fiers de toi.* I'm proud of you.

Up the next morning, we do our usual romp in the chateau grounds. Back for coffee and a trip to the boulangerie.

At the event in Cognac I realized it was time to move from field events to the field itself. Clearly Marcel had flair and *flaire* both. In our commune, the hunters were already assembling on weekend mornings, working the fields around our village and beyond.

I would place myself among those not native French who are surprised to learn how keen they are on guns and hunting. One local offered that before the Revolution, the only people generally allowed to have guns were royalty (think the owners of the chateau where we lived) and soldiers. All that changed in 1789. Farmers who might well have owned guns in the south of France were now joined by the wider citizenry anxious to be able to have firearms for self-protection and the clearing of pesky birds attacking their fields, hogs, and roe deer.

From the hunting on horseback done by upper classes, or the driven hog and deer clearing organized for them, or the shooting of imported pheasants, now we have seasonal hunting by the citizenry of the communes. You know it is underway as signs are posted on Montgomery's forest road linking Fontainebleau (and the Anglican chapel there) with our home twenty minutes away in Courances. *Chasse en cours* they read, with a big hog-snouted face in case your French isn't too good. Hunt in progress. You see these same signs all over France in the fall and through the winter months.

I will learn that the procedure is to gather on Saturday (and Sunday, but not for me) mornings at a location posted at the Marie. There is a farm outside of our village as you climb the hill, and I know the road and place well. It is on my afternoon bike route. In fact, it is an assembly of barns and hangars for farm equipment and tractors, with a big area where you can park. Our commune group consists of about eight, with their various dogs.

The mayor of our town is a good-natured Portuguese woman whose brother-in-law is the enthusiastic organizer of the hunts. (There was a big influx of Portuguese into France during the Salazar dictatorship in the earlier twentieth century.) Famous as stonemasons (among other things), they were in much demand at places like the chateau of Courances. Our housekeeper Maria and her husband Adelino were proud *portugais.* He is in charge of our property outdoors and Elizabeth's transformation of the garden.

I was always struck at the Fête Nationale ceremony or kindred public events in front of the Marie, how many Portuguese would be present. They were extremely proud French citizens, the country to which they had fled for refuge and which had welcomed them and taken them in. Also at our Catholic church, their favorite saint's days were celebrated with gusto. Street processions with statues of the Virgin, singing, big family gatherings, colorful outfits.

The hunts would consist of birds in the fields in the morning and hogs and roe deer in the forests in the afternoon, our Portuguese leader explained. He explained the *déroulement*, though it was pretty straightforward. When the time would come, I would just hunt in the mornings. Marcel is too powerful to control if he starts coursing hogs, and it would be dangerous in my view. Elizabeth forbade it, and that settled that.

I would need to get Marcel a bit more training, I felt. Friends in Cognac recommended the trainer *numero uno* in France, if not in continental Europe. As Filson outfitters say, "Might as well have the best." His name was Emmanuel Bourgeois. His operation was in Lower Normandy, a hilly and woody section known as Le Perche, presently favored by Parisians because it is easy to get to for weekends in the country.

His business was known as *Les Buveurs d'Air*. Air-drinkers, literally. Marcel had proven he was a very good *buveur d'air* at the championship in Cognac. Now I needed to be able to control him in the field, and around other dogs, off lead.

Off he would go for two weeks in November. Meanwhile, I had my own training to do if I was to get the required *permis de chasse*, the hunting license necessary to hunt and also to buy a gun in France.

25

La Chasse

LE PERCHE IS IN the Eure-et-Loire Departement. It is an ancient name like Berry or Gâtinais, where Courances is located. M. Bourgeois's *Buveurs d'Air* (literally, "air/scent drinkers") is in the small farm village of Thiron-Gardais, a bit under two hours away by car.

We have made arrangements with him by phone. Since he comes so highly regarded, we don't feel it necessary to inspect the place. He has described his routines. Mr. Best Dog Trainer Around doesn't talk a lot. He's just back from an important dog event in Hungary. He's talked to dogs so much I suspect that talking to people is something he's forgotten how to do. I picked up that same sense when I arrive and meet him. We humans have our own *flaire* (scent).

It is a spiffy facility. He shows me where Marcel will stay. It's outdoors and the weather is getting cold at night. Other than that, things look good. His training stint will be two weeks. I pass through le Croix du Perche as I head back and notice a beautiful small church. I will stop by when I return to get him.

Back home I am working on my hunting license. All the sample questions are online. This is the written part. Someone came up with the clever idea to make a test about hunting also a test to see if you are the best ornithologist, ecologist, all-around expert on flora and fauna in France. This takes us into a vocabulary terrain I suspect most average French citizens would struggle with.

When the X type deer loses its horns, how long before the next set appear? Can you fire a gun over sea water in Y conditions. How many litters can a lynx have in a year? What breed of elk are found in France?

These predominate over, Can you fire a shotgun toward power lines? At what angle can you fire if shooting hogs on a line, with gun wielding neighbors on right and left? What's the difference between buckshot and double 00? How many départments in France allow air-propelled guns for shooting rats and other vermin?

This is all very cleverly thought through. There are on the order of 350 such questions, I kid you not. For the exam, you only get twenty, chosen at random. There is one question—usually fairly obvious—about gun safety that, if you miss, the exam is forfeited. The online format is perfect. You can test yourself as many times as you like with an exam just like the one you must take at the formal training and license facility. The closest one to me is in the Seine-et-Marne Department, about twenty minutes to the northeast, beyond Melun. I sit in my mezzanine office and enjoy the challenge for a half-hour each day. My paperback copy of the questions arrives in the post.

We are having a cold snap and nighttime temperatures are down into the low thirties. Marcel's outdoor sleeping place arises in my mind's eye, a concrete cell in French Siberia. Elizabeth is also worried. She insists I call M. Dresseur. He answers his cell phone in his usual brusque manner, as if he were in the middle of negotiating a 5M deal between France and Belarus. Will Marcel be OK? It's pretty cold at night.

He's a hunting dog. *Chien de chasse*. He'll get used to it.

End of call.

I go back to taking the sample test and studying the video that came with the book. It shows how the practical part of the exam will unfold. You also can go up for some face-to-face instruction. They have the guns that are part of the exam when the time comes to take it. In the weeks before the actual formal exam, there are several weekends where groups are walked through the practical exam.

I have been hunting since a boy, in rural Western North Carolina. We shot dove in fields around my boarding school. I have shot migrating and local ducks from a blind and boat in South Carolina. I was invited to some exciting shoots in Perthshire in Scotland when I lived in St. Andrews.

All that said, I genuinely like the idea of this kind of thorough training, as it socializes the would-be hunters to the basics and lets one learn alongside others. I have never breached a shotgun in the way required for the French exam, and I have not shot semi-automatic shotguns in the field as a rule, though they are very popular. They make you break down and put back together these weapons, as well as a basic bolt-action rifle typically used for hog and deer hunts. This is where you learn about proper minimal angles of shooting for driven hogs and deer, which is the usual way departmentally organized clearing exercises—*chasse en cours*—take place.

The day for the exam, written and practical, arrives. We've gotten to know each other, test-takers and instructors. I did not want to repeat the rookie experience I had at a field trial. I didn't. I passed the written exam with the required 80 percent correct. The practical exam was a bit harder, but I think the examiner knew my age and history of hunting made me an acceptable pass. That this is not a cakewalk is proven by the fact that routinely only 65 percent pass on the first go. If you fail, you study and come back, now more familiar with the process. I like my shiny embossed *permis de chasse.* Locals in our village who know about these things are impressed that I passed on my first trial.

I have left my own shotguns at home, but that's a nice excuse to find a suitable 20 gauge to augment my array of "fowling pieces." There is a nice gun shop south of Fontainebleau. "Might as well have the best" comes to mind. Instead, I find a moderately priced brand I have seen promoted. FAIR. Fabricio armi Italiano Rimini. Nice etchings on the face. Looks like Marcel at point. I produce my hunting permit, pay, and we are off. I've bought shells for various weight birds we will be shooting, and some slugs in case the afternoon hunts come into play.

Speaking of Marcel. When it was time for him to come home, I was happy to get our buddy back. Elizabeth really missed him. He loves curling up at her feet in our cozy living room, especially in this colder season. And she loves it too.

M. Bourgeois is in the field when I arrive, and he signals for me to come. He has said that his favorite dogs to work with are English pointers, Braque d'Anglais. They can take a lot of discipline, and it doesn't bother them. He finds Marcel's breed a challenge. They work the field very well. But they are also a challenging combination of stubborn and sensitive. He tells me Marcel has done fine. But he wants me to be aware of this.

As I watch, he gives Marcel a command. Marcel reacts a bit slowly. He is stropped once on his rump. Then he gets a huge hug. I am to do the same thing. They need discipline, he says. They are stubborn and a bit independent. *Tétu* (headstrong). But their spirit can't be crushed. Immediate affection is required.

Why does that sound a lot like life?

This little exercise came prior to settling the bill and leaving. Before that, he had me stand downwind so he could show me Marcel at work in the field. Marcel was not to know I was there. There is something touching about seeing the dog you love, who operates always in your orbit, step out of that and be himself. He is Marcel. His own dog. He is doing what God gave him to do, that rises from within him naturally, now just more disciplined, chiseled, crisp, and efficient. Emmanuel put him through his paces and is done. He signals for me, and I step into the field.

With his now customary squeal and whine at the sight of me and those he loves, he runs to me across the field. This is the hug part we all long for in life.

He's in his car now, his mobile home, going back to see his *maman*. Now it's her turn to give the mom's version of a squeal and a whine. Followed by a hug.

"You're home, Marcel," she says. "I have a treat for you."

26

Winter Arrives in Courances

Marcel and I would join the local hunters for the season's start. He is not just a capable dog, but a highly efficient pointer and well-disciplined. We would get light snows from time to time, which made things even more romantic. I can see him by his pile of birds in the courtyard of le Presbytère, looking up to have his picture taken. Exhausted. I sent a photo to my brother and he said he looks "plumb tuckered out." In French, *vanné, crevé, rincé.*

The gift-wrapped boxes were again at the *maternelle* (nursery school, kindergarten) next to the Marie, just as they had been when we arrived from Dallas a year ago. What a year. What a year. All the chores, and adventures, and settling in, and French Affaires, and TAN, and new friends, and Mass in Milly, and our new Anglican church, and our new home at 7 rue du petit Paris. The guests that flocked to our door. So many beautiful memories. We would be off shortly to the prefecture in Evry to renew our *Titre de Séjour* (visa). We were enrolled in the excellent French healthcare system, knew the pharmacy, hair salon, doctors and nurses, best restaurants, favorite hiking trails, favorite weekend getaways.

We were at home now. Elizabeth's garden was dormant for the winter but would spring into life in late March. The new roof and refurbishment of my office *maisonette* had been completed. The wood furnace puts out an amazing amount of heat. We have a garage space full of seasoned wood and Elizabeth has me on fireplace duty. It is all very efficient. Twenty paces to the wood pile and back to replenish our big living room fireplace.

We have decided to put on a Lessons and Carols service next door at St. Etienne. My new private prayer church! The French love carol singing. English carols are characteristically thought of as the quintessence of the Christmas season. *Il est né le petit enfant* is also hard to beat. We decide on a mixture of English and French hymns, and lessons to be read in both languages. Père Mercier will officiate with me of course. The mayor will send out notices.

Because of the separation of church and state, there is no singing of carols in the schools, so this comes as a welcome offering. The French equivalent of the Trapp Family Singers happens to be in our parish, and they will bring their talents, mother on the guitar and three gorgeous young voices.

Patrick's wife Isabelle pitches in and makes lovely bulletins for the service, with red yarn as the binding. Elizabeth will prepare a mulled wine for the event, which wafts through the ancient church, to be served at the back when we have concluded.

Of course we must get a Christmas tree!

Elizabeth has been busy decking the house, each window supplied with its own battery-powered candle with wreath at base. This is her "season to be jolly." The little girl from Highland Park creating a French home at Christmas. Pull out all the stops. Favorite Christmas music from early December on.

We see a super "Christmas tree for sale" place, set up on the right side of the roundabout as you leave Fontainebleau, after we depart from Sunday morning Anglican church services. Yes, the French can be garish, too! We will head back mid-week. Our station wagon ought to be able to comfortably handle any holiday tree. We are, to be sure, in the Forest of Fontainebleau, and Christmas tree farms thrive in our region and climate. Elizabeth has goosebumps. The final missing piece of Christmas *au Presbytère*.

We are back home and having lunch. We'll head back out to the Christmas tree place as it looks like a major enterprise and where most people buy their trees. Come on, Marcel, should be exciting. Your first Christmas!

We arrive and the place is humming. Now, Elizabeth and I had celebrated Christmas at our home in Dallas, of course, and I knew something of her taste in trees. This place was Christmas Tree Central, however, and the sizes ran from medium to grand. "Grand" is where Elizabeth always goes. I complain I'm not sure it will fit in the house. Oh, calm down. Of course it will.

Grand it will be.

When it comes time to load the thing, I back the station wagon up for them to place it in. Marcel is there so we leash him for the operation. Of course there is not enough room. But the deed is done, and Elizabeth has the we-shall-make-this-work look on her face. In the tree goes, top bit first. All the way up to the inside windscreen and bending a bit upon arrival. Can't close the station wagon door. Not a problem, they tied the gate in some inventive way. As for Marcel? He will ride in the front seat with Elizabeth. I am dubious, she is thrilled, Marcel is confused. Why is there a tree in our car? Trees are for marking.

Mental note on that, when we get back to *le Presbytère* and get the tree positioned in the corner of the living room.

At least we have double wide gates and doors, so the importation process yields up only a modest bunch of cursing. We had opted for them to put a nice wooden base on the trunk, since that was a small additional price and we didn't move a Christmas tree holder with us to France. We would discover reasonably quickly why these holders are important. Yes, these trees need water. The very ancient looking and traditional stands are nicely ancient and traditional, but that is because your average person putting up a tree in the nineteenth century and earlier didn't have it in the house for two weeks. We will put up with the dropped needles this year, and next year plump for the stand associated with the twenty-first-century Christmas-tree realities.

How grand the house looks with the tree full of lights. We have a big red oriental rug that fills the room and that too feels like Christmas, offset by all the greenery filling the windows. We have snow outside and carols on the Bose player. It is December dark, with short days and long nights. The fires go all day in the fireplace, and in the morning I have simply to stir the embers and reload. The house was made to let the fireplaces do their work. We have one in our bedroom as well, but it isn't necessary. Our home is a sanctuary of Christmas warmth, kitchen smells, a resplendent tree, lights in the window, and joy in the heart. Move over, Currier and Ives.

The evening comes for our well-advertised Lessons and Carols service. A keyboard player comes from the Milly parish. We have the "Trapp Family." And we have a church packed and ready to sing in French and in English. Members of the parishes nearby have joined us. And the citizens of our little village we don't usually see on Sundays. And surprise, the

Marquise and her two sons and one daughter are there, she now being helped to walk. It feels like the entire village and our neighbors have come together to sing in a Joyeux Noël.

I will never forget this evening. All the hands that helped make it work. Paul-Marie and me leading the simple service. And, of course, the final "Silent Night." Sung without accompaniment, each person now waiting for the candles distributed at the start to be lit. The acolytes come down the aisle with tapers. The lights are extinguished.

It is a foretaste of heaven.

Then the lights come back on, and I see Elizabeth standing by a huge punch bowl—product of her *brocante* searches—ready to ladle hot mulled wine into plastic cups. *C'est vin chaud*, I hear her strong teacher's voice announce. Mulled wine.

Joyeux Noël. Merry Christmas one and all.

I think of the words of John Betjeman. I recite them from memory each Christmas.

> And is it true and is it true
> This most tremendous tale of all
> Seen in a stained-glass window's hue
> A Baby in an ox's stall?
> The maker of the stars and sea
> Become a child on earth for me?
>
> And is it true for if it is
> No loving fingers tying strings
> Around those tissued fripperies
> Bath salts, inexpensive scent
> And hideous tie so kindly meant.
>
> No love that in a family dwells
> No caroling in frosty air
> Nor all the steeple shaking bells
> Can with this simple truth compare.
>
> That God was man in Palestine
> And lives today in bread and wine.

Merry Christmas one and all.

Elizabeth and I are in our home, in our church, in our village, and Marcel has joined the fun. The party is complete.

Our first Christmas and one that will live forever in our memory.

Škoda
Škoda
Carrefour
Carrefour
Carrefour

Conclusion

I HAVE CHOSEN TO limit the episodes for this retelling so most of them fit within a single year. That provides a loose framework, though I obviously speak of things prior to this calendar year and after it. I have not wanted to follow a chronological line, but rather to move into different regions to keep the widest palette for painting the riches of France. In the case of Marcel, I have conflated parts of 2016 and later episodes that happened in the following year. He was a year older than appears here when undertaking the road to TAN success and his training in *le Perche*.

I could easily double the episodes. Elizabeth and I lived in France a bit over four years, full time. We travelled widely in the five years prior to our long sojourn in Courances. We have travelled since. French Affaires continues to take excited travelers to France. Its riches, regions, long history, and culture cannot be exhausted.

In the Scriptures we hear of being born again. Because the Holy Spirit does this work, many and varied would be the accounts individuals might give of how that work took hold of them and changed them. The Spirit blows where the Spirit wills. It is like the wind you cannot see but only hear the outskirts of. Yet the destination is the same. Becoming a new creation, at God's hand, sometimes with our permission and at other times when our wills are depleted and spent, and choosing itself has ceased making much sense.

For all the years and all the wonderful times that Elizabeth and I spent in France, the single year I write about here is special. Unique. I have thought about why that is so.

I believe it is tied up with things I said in passing about learning a new language. You are asked to become a child again and start over, now with the language you know a help and a hindrance to learning to live in one you don't. A baby crawls before walking and then stumbles before standing, and in time running and dancing and frolicking. A first year in France retains a very special quality.

Elizabeth of course speaks French well enough for it to approach her "mother tongue." That does not dampen all the myriad ways she and I had to learn a new language. Church, healthcare, kennel, maps, currency, food, roofing, hiking trails, hunting, buying food and wine, bakeries, autoroute pay stations, pet stores, hogs snorting in French, bunkers on the beach, arms folded and voices quiet at a verse sung in German, operation escargot and Uber strike, *Titre de Séjour* renewal, *permis de chasse*, post office, police, and parking. A big iron key opening a small green wooden gate, a world of wonder behind it. *Vas-y Marcel.*

Dogs are not born again because every day they are a new creation of wonder.

I recall sitting in church and listening to a service conducted in a language Elizabeth could follow and that I had to learn to follow. But in many ways, what was going on penetrated that part of us that seeks to soar and love and forgive and confess and be made new. And I believe this was more so because things were unfamiliar, were cut off from the things we know and take for granted, until we have lost our sense of childhood and awe and fear. Confusion becoming understanding. Prose becoming song.

Le grand voyage is how I think of this. When Jacques Brel wrote the lyrics to his famous ballad, *Quand on n'a que l'amour*, the first stanza speaks of offering to each other a form of sharing unique to love. Elizabeth and I did that. He called it "the day of the grand voyage, that is our *grand amour.*" It may not feel that way at the time, but it is in sharing the life of a grand voyage that one discovers a grand love. That is why it is important to recall it, as I have sought to do in these pages.

Here we see the conspiracy at work between learning a new language amid the languages we know, and learning it alongside another, such that we both are born anew.

A year tinged with heaven.

Interlude

I WILL CONTINUE DOWN the lanes that Elizabeth and I shared, as I share our France with travelers at French Affaires, the company she founded. The company that founded our life on *le grand voyage*. As I mention above, I limit the opening chapters on that journey to a single calendar year, to make the movement light and brisk, rich and joyous. As it was.

We stayed in France for a further three years, and the roads we went down and the adventures we shared continued. Marcel became a fixture at the hunts in our village. He is stubborn and brilliant in two languages.

I shared a flavor of the present work with a colleague I work with in the Var region of Provence. The phrase *le grand voyage*, she told me, has an extended nuance among the French. It is the voyage through life and into death and beyond.

Elizabeth and I moved to France in 2016 for one main reason. Shortly into our marriage, she was diagnosed with a rare pulmonary condition called LAM disease. It is akin to cancer, but with its own definitive signature, as it attacks the lung tissues. There is no known cure. After the National Institute of Health could do no more, we moved to France.

For the first part of this book, I wanted to tell the story of France that Elizabeth would want me to write. A story in which LAM disease receded because France was arriving with its grace, beauty, and joy, making this terminal disease far less central than if we had remained in the United States. A year tinged with heavenly grace.

The stories I have shared are true stories in the best sense of the word. They convey the inner heart of our time together, undampened by disease or worry. They tell the truth about Elizabeth and me and "A Life Lived Well in France."

I now want to tell the story of France with LAM present.

In *As I Lay Dying*, William Faulkner told a simple story through the different angles of vision those sharing it saw and were then conveyed at his hand. One effect of that is like holding a rare gem to the light and shifting it in one's grasp so that the refractions combine and tell us what we are seeing. Rich and rare things require that kind of handling.

I now move to the second part of the story called simply "A Breath of French Air." The title was Elizabeth's choice. She was the one who would have her life returned to her. New breath in new French lungs sown into her body.

This "breath of French air" would become true and life-saving language about what we shared on this segment of the grand voyage.

For the reader to understand the flow of the book as it unfolds, I should say that the present Part Two was composed to chronicle a journey from terminal disease to victory. It was written first, a year after the Paris surgery that saved her life, snatching her from the jaws of death. It was written in the joyous awareness that "A Life Lived Well in France," though shadowed by disease, was a life lived well, undaunted and strong all the same. That is why Part One reads as it does.

Elizabeth would never let the disease diagnosed two years into our marriage get in the way of the life that would, after five years in the United States, be ours in France. So, I have written Part One in the way I have because she would not have wanted it otherwise. And I would not have wanted it otherwise. You can hear that in what I have written. Our rich and rare life in a small village in France.

I will now, in the chapters to follow, chapters that I wrote first, allow the reality of terminal disease to enter the stage. I believe it is best to do that through the lens, the vestibule, of the joyous year I have chronicled thus far.

For that reality—a life lived well—always weighed greater than anything we would be asked to go through. It shines through undiminished, and is what carried us resolutely along.

When we talk about life and death, the linear character of time ceases to be a dominant reality. I have wanted to leave undisturbed, as far as possible, the account I wrote first, now to follow, even when prefaced by the chapters in Part One, written later. I have tried to make this transition work in the form you read them, where these two parts sit astride one another. The latter and the former, the former and the latter, conjoined in the form being presented.

I have left some overlap on purpose, because this remains true to these two dimensions of our life. "A Life Lived Well in France" on the passage to "A Breath of French Air." When I refer to dates, it is done within the time frame of the writing of the materia, and not this present time.

Now, then, we embark on this part of *Le Grand Voyage*. Life-saving breath in lungs that had been invaded by a genetic condition and its eventual fallout, unknown to her or me, slowly killing her if not somehow stopped.

This section of the grand voyage took her and me as close to death as is possible in this life. It is where our life would be changed. As only trial will do. Reshaped forever.

Part Two

A Breath of French Air

Preface

THE STORY TO UNFOLD in this section will take you on a journey. From a woman with marathon-runner health to one with hours to live and in the jaws of death. It ends with survival against all odds, in the hands of experts at saving lives. It is a story of endurance, decline, despair, friendship, prayers, courage, lost hope, and regained stamina. It ends in a victory hard-won and depleting, a miracle in a Paris hospital bed and surgical theater. It is a story of transplanted life.

It is a story of two people, a husband and wife, on a journey into uncharted territory. Both will speak here. Chris almost lost a wife. Elizabeth almost lost her life.

We were of course accompanied by family, friends, fellow-travelers, priests, brave nurses, medical researchers, and peerless surgeons. The journey crossed Dallas hospitals, Toronto clinics, the National Institute of Health, *Hôpital Kremlin Bicêtre* in Paris, and reached its final stopping point by helicopter across rush-hour Paris, landing at *l'Hôpital Marie Lannelounge* transplant hospital. And the journey also includes our French pointer companion, Marcel, always patient, compassionate, and somehow understanding. The long oxygen tubes trailing through our French home he negotiated like a champ to stay close to his *maîtresse*.

Out of the blue, in the fall of 2011, Elizabeth was diagnosed with an extremely rare lung disease called LAM, an acronym for the unpronounceable Lymphangiolieomyomatosis. The thoracic specialist who sought to diagnose her early symptoms could barely recall the disease from his medical training, so rare is it. It entails lymph deterioration and blockage of air within the lungs. There is no known cure and, as we learned, no single agreed method of treatment. The NIH is hard at work on LAM as I write, and they and their international colleagues track cases and consult one another regularly.

This is also a story inextricably rooted in France, for that is where the most intense years of the journey played out. Looking back on it now, we can both recall an unusual shortness of breath Elizabeth experienced in the summer of 2011, hiking in the Pyrenees outside of St. Jean Pied de Port. So wherever and whenever the disease began taking root, our sense of its impact began in France and would end there.

Now, some years ago the law in France was changed to enable organ transplant from anyone who has died, unless one formally requests not to be a donor. It is our conviction she would not have lived long enough for a suitable transplant to save her life had we not been in France and had we not been enrolled in their excellent healthcare system. More of that story will be told below. But it is important as an explanation for the title of this section of the book, as well as for our profound sense of gratitude to France, to state this right up front.

After she was sufficiently stable and the imminent danger of death had passed, I would joke that having mastered the French language, her life's work, she was now borrowing French body parts. Elizabeth's travel, culture, and language business, French Affaires, took her and us to France, and showing France to Americans is the joy and purpose of her life. France cannot have given more in return, for they have given back to her, *en fait*, in fact, her very life.

In the middle of an ordeal like this, one will search about for the reasons. Why me? Why us? Why my wife? Maybe the reason is the account we will set before you here, now on the other side of the valley of the shadow of death.

1

Hard News

I MET MY WIFE in church. She was ten years younger than me. She was wearing gorgeous French stockings of the kind you cannot pull off unless you are Elizabeth New, and they did what they are supposed to do—set her apart. Smart, pretty, strong, don't-mess-with-Texas femininity. I'd now say French–Texas elegance.

I was fifty-five at the time and not yet married. What are the odds at my age of finding someone like Elizabeth, who was also single? Career had been my life, and I had also lived in academic settings where day-to-day life is harder to find and to enjoy. Yale for ten years, St. Andrews in Scotland for another ten. And twenty years of graduate education and publishing just to get at the point of tenure security amid those two professional academic decades.

It was somewhat awkward to court her, because I was also the priest associate on the staff of the church where we met. Lots of ways that could go wrong. But it didn't. We even had kindly parishioner friends seek to set us up, not knowing God had done that already.

I was teaching PhD students in Toronto at the time, but in a research professorship that allowed me to be present in the classroom less frequently. This is our age of intensive terms, the internet, and Skype (now Zoom et al.). I had moved to Dallas to help launch a satellite campus there and serve as teacher-theologian at a big downtown parish church. After one mid-week lecture session, this intelligent and pretty woman came up to ask me a question.

We dated for a bit less than a year, traveled to her home away from home, France, visiting Paris and Provence. She visited me in Toronto.

We decided to get married. My dad is a priest, and he did the wedding, a small event for close friends and family. We honeymooned in the Dordogne region of France, attending Christmas Mass at Rocamadour, and then flew to Scotland for a week in my old home of St. Andrews, staying at the Old Course Hotel.

The next summer I got licensed to serve in the Church of England's Diocese in Europe and took services in the Medoc for five weeks. It was that summer when we visited St. Jean Pied de Port. I had passed through the village thirty-five years earlier en route to Pamplona, and on the footsteps of Ernest Hemingway, like many young men of my age. Elizabeth the marathon-runner seemed to be oddly out of breath on occasion. We put it down to altitude and forgot it.

A year passed in our new house and new rhythms. The following summer we were in Toronto for one of my teaching stints. Elizabeth jogged in Queen's Park but something was slowing her usual pace and stamina.

In the fall of that same year, I left to teach again in Toronto. Elizabeth was to join me, flying up later from our Dallas home. I had found a nice rental apartment during the summer, and it would be a bit more comfortable than other short-term lodgings I had found before. I got a call that her doctor had found a lung issue he was not sure how to evaluate. That scared me, of course.

I am a professional biblical scholar and an ordained clergyman. My father, grandfather, two uncles, and two brothers are or were ordained clergy, and the church has been my only home, spiritually and literally. I consider myself a mature Christian.

But when one enrolls in the school of disease and decline and the unknown and the threat of death, no one is a master and everyone is a student. Diseases like LAM are great levelers.

I have taught the book of Job a dozen times and have written what I consider essays full of insight. Pain and fear are teachers like no other, and God uses them and allows them to speak their peculiar language. The Psalms speak of the writhing of our insides, of bottles of tears, and of palpable dread. This would be the territory and terrain that Elizabeth and I were about to enter.

2

Slow Decline

THE ORIGINS OF LAM disease and the reasons for it are unknown. Doctors do not agree on how to treat its uncomfortable symptoms, as the lungs fill up with lymph fluid from day to day and make breathing hard and life uncomfortable. One can remove the fluid by various means, but the vacuum created is just as quickly replaced by new fluid. Plus, the fluid is rich in nutrients, so depleting it means depleting the patient.

The thoracic specialist recommended to us in Dallas had treated several people with LAM, which put him in a category as rare as the disease itself. Elizabeth started a regime that involved a tube surgically implanted that served to drain the lymph fluid. The tube reached from her spine area where it connected inside to the lung cavity and came around to her tummy on her front side. This was done so she could personally attach a second set of tubes and a vacuum bottle and, following the procedures for sanitizing the spout, drain off liters of fluid into bottles. All the bits of the apparatus for this being ordered, they would arrive by FedEx at regular shipments.

None of this inspired much confidence, of course. It was awkward, messy, tedious, and only temporarily addressed a problem—breathlessness—which was not going away. Our life was taking place in Dallas, Toronto, and France—or so we had been living it—and the bottle routine was no compact traveling show.

Prior to the vacuum bottles, in the early days of her diagnosis, Elizabeth came to visit me in Toronto. Day by day she was getting short of breath. To use the subway, one had to know whether there was an up-escalator or an elevator. Simple routines of shopping or getting out to walk became fraught with complication.

For reasons I do not fully recall, it was clear she needed to go to the emergency room and be attended to. I mention this in the present context because it illustrates the problems LAM presents. It is so rare even specialists do not know what to do. We got referred to the best and brightest—and Toronto is the center of superb medical research—and entered a shiny hospital for treatment. After endless questioning about a disease we knew better firsthand than they did, and the reasons for her needing care, a doctor tentatively inserted a catheter so as to drain a good portion of fluid off. You get this wrong and you have punctured an already sick lung. Successfully executed, it helped a bit yet anticipated the problems we would encounter when this became a daily routine. It is only a very short-term help.

We knew we needed to get her back to Dallas to meet with the specialist there and dig further into treatments for a longer road ahead. Once you "solve" the immediate problem with a catheter and draining, you then create conditions tricky or impossible for air travel and compression in the cabin. So, you are almost literally stuck between a rock and a hard place.

It was finally counseled that we take the risk—it is a long way by ground transport from Toronto to Dallas—to get her back to Dallas and daily care as quickly as possible. The severity of her condition was now no longer a fact we could hide from, or hope wasn't all that bad.

You will likely have caught on, too, that this kind of a health condition isn't simply a matter of physical discomfort. Sensing that you cannot breathe is a bit like drowning, and it triggers anxiety in its wake. This, in turn, affects breathing, and so a spiral of mental and emotional stress mixes up with the physical problem itself. Throw in that one has a disease no one really understands very well, or knows how to treat or what to expect, even in the offices of obvious experts, and LAM starts showing its peculiar teeth.

We all in time come to accept that medical experts are just that and deserve our highest respect. It is another thing to maintain that high respect, and properly so, when one begins to peer behind the curtain and realize diseases are experts too, and have their own cunning and resolve. This did not lower our respect one bit for our physician, as we saw a tremendously highly trained expert struggle honestly and courageously and lovingly with just what to do. Months were passing. The bottles arrived, were filled up, and disposed of, and new ones arrived to take up where they had left off. But it was obvious this could go on indefinitely and it was not making progress but was only a form of treading water. Treading that is exhausting and that begins to have other knock-on effects.

One of the realities of a slow decline like this, without a clear sense of how things might improve, is that the world begins to close in. It is hard to pay attention to things that one once loved and did reflexively, just as part and parcel of daily life. LAM begins to be, not ironically, suffocating.

When this happened, then other things began to unravel. The satellite campus idea was fraught with NAFTA tangles and concerns and so it had to be shelved. But far worse and not at all expected, our health insurance coverage became an issue. Churches are of course meant to be special places, but they, too, have business managers and healthcare costs to monitor. LAM disease, given its character, its possible duration, its rarity and seeming intractability will worry employers and underwriters. It would require a steady hand and a commitment to see one through, and it was becoming clear these were not in place.

We were fortunate that others in the diocese were alert to our dilemma and committed to continue our healthcare. But the shock of this reality remains to this day. One can get terribly sick, not see the way forward medically, and then lose whatever healthcare support one assumed would be rock solid.

A further challenge was not being able to convey the seriousness of the disease. No one need know about the daily bottle procedures and the specialist's stymied efforts to find a way forward. Life and work marched on, Elizabeth did not look too bad, people lead busy lives, and disease is unpleasant, especially when so rare and unheard of as LAM. Clergy are meant to give help, not receive it, or at least not over a long haul and without any obvious remedy. I suspect that was a further reason for creating a situation that would require us to move on.

And this is a time when true friends reveal their worth and patience and loyalty. They come out of the woodwork.

We also had to search for some special cases of help. I am more of an extravert that Elizabeth. She is a private woman enduring a private and largely invisible daily assault on her breathing and her life. At my urging, she reached out and found a LAM network. A phone call was arranged. A woman in Boston with LAM agreed to talk with Elizabeth, to bring some fresh air into the suffocating and hard isolation she was enduring.

This led to Elizabeth being referred to the National Institute of Health in Bethesda, Maryland. The NIH researches diseases and cures for them, especially intractable ones. LAM was and is rare, but it had become sufficiently widespread that it qualified for their dedicated efforts to get to the bottom of the disease. A team of scientific research experts and treating physicians received her in January of 2012. This would be the start of a new episode in the journey before us.

3

Off to Experts

ELIZABETH WOULD BE THE better storyteller on this phase of our journey, as she was the main actor in the NIH work to unfold. She would be their research patient for four solid years. She visited them for several days to weeks on numerous occasions during this period, before we moved to France in late 2015. I had hoped she would write her account, but that would not transpire, as it turned out.

Elizabeth's research team, physicians, and nurses were trying to break the code of this disease and were working, and had been, tirelessly and diligently, for decades, with LAM patients from all over the US. But they also became her fathers, mothers, sisters, and brothers. One can speak of a LAM family and mean just that, all bearing the trials and disappointments together, and together seeking the hopes of healing and a way forward, whatever that might take.

Life of course goes on. The LAM disease was going nowhere fast, but there was a measure of stability that comes from doing the tasks required by the illness and putting one foot in front of the other. I had my PhD students to teach and supervise and my writing schedule to attend to.

Elizabeth continued to build her life's love, French Affaires, LLC.

In the summer of 2012, we spent several months in a small, rented cottage at the foot of Les Baux-de-Provence. *La Serre* (the greenhouse) was a converted three-room villa that had previously served as a storage place for plants during the winter months. Placed in the middle of an olive grove and nestled below the majestic range of the historic site known as Les Baux-de-Provence, Elizabeth could rest while I worked on a writing project: a commentary on the Epistle to the Colossians.

The best feature of Provence in the summer is the regularity of the weather. Blue skies, no humidity, little to no rain, warm days, and cool nights: a steady state that helped assure us during our LAM struggle. The NIH had increased the medications they were experimenting with to fight LAM and their benefits were clear. I could take long daily walks to clear my mind and compose my next writing thoughts, and we could together enjoy long summer lunches of salade niçoise and famous Côte du Rhone rosé.

We love a place that is familiar to us, and the St. Remy, Maussane, Les Baux, Eygalières, Avignon corridor is that. Arlès, Fontvielle, Uzès and Pont du Gard offer charming places to visit close-by, and Aix-en-Provence and Cassis a bit further on. Elizabeth did graduate work in Aix, so it comes with fond memories of a healthy youth. We have a Dallas friend who summers at the foot of Mt. Ventoux, famous for the Tour de France cyclists, in the small village of Crillon le Brave. We always enjoy our time there and in the Luberon range below her home.

We returned to Dallas refreshed and I was proud to have finished my writing. Editing would come next, but the main hard work was behind me. We returned to the blow that our healthcare was ending, and as said, this was a jolt from the blue we had not anticipated.

Elizabeth continued her regular visits to Bethesda, where they monitored her condition and regulated her medications. As 2013 approached, she would have been suffering from LAM for sixteen months. The way forward and out from under the disease was no clearer. A Google search will reveal strings like "there is no cure for LAM" and "most treatments for LAM are aimed at easing symptoms and preventing complications." So it seemed to us as well.

It was about this time that a surgical procedure called a pleurodesis was discussed as a way to make some advance. It is "a procedure that uses medicine to adhere your lung to your chest wall. It seals up the space between the outer lining of your lung and chest wall (pleural cavity) to prevent fluid or air from continually building up around your lungs." There is however a significant downside. It can address some of the discomfort LAM patients experience, but it does not do anything to resolve the disease itself. If in time a lung transplant becomes necessary, a pleurodesis will create serious challenges for a successful surgery. Indeed, it will likely make it impossible.

Where there was widespread agreement among NIH experts involved the tube-draining system that had been introduced to help

Elizabeth breathe. The medicine sirolimus is meant to attack the lymph fluid build-up on its own and help the body do its own fighting. The draining was nutritionally harmful, but it was also not working well in conjunction with the preferred treatment of the NIH team. And as one might have suspected of such a long period of using it—approaching two years—it was a perfect home for attracting infection, no matter how religiously one did the sanitizing necessaries. I have never met someone as diligent as my wife.

I was away celebrating my brother's fiftieth birthday in Scotland when it became clear the NIH would need to surgically remove the draining tubes. Elizabeth would have to undergo that procedure alone, and it was not easy. But in general, we were aware that sirolimus and a pleurodesis option and perhaps a transplant were not attractive realities to have in mind. And, as Google will also say candidly about LAM, ten years of life expectancy is not unusual. It is a terminal disease.

For the next three years we found a way to live with the sirolimus treatments and the limitations LAM was imposing on Elizabeth's movements. I got an Alexander von Humboldt research award, and we spent three nice months in Göttingen, Germany. I finished a commentary on the book of Joel there. Superb public transportation is a blessing. We attended an annual von Humboldt event in Berlin and had the pleasure of meeting the president of Germany at his lovely estate. We visited Luther sites and the former East Germany. We took advantage of being in Europe and drove south to our favorite destination, Provence.

All this time, Elizabeth was trying to keep her mind and soul active by focusing on her French Affaires business. I went to Aix the following summer with one of her groups and did a French immersion course. We would reconnoiter the distances and routes ahead of time. This would become a regular routine now, wherever we were.

The regular visits to the NIH continued and the specialists tried to sound hopeful, but we knew the clock was ticking. Elizabeth was slowly worsening. Her oxygen density, monitored several times a day, gave the hard reality. A pleurodesis was becoming ever more necessary, even with the dangers that attended it. We attended a wedding in Bourron-Marlotte, south of Fontainebleau. I began thinking that, if Elizabeth was not going to have long to live, perhaps we could spend the final years in the France she loved and that was her life's work.

She had made the many trips to Bethesda, Maryland, and the NIH facility there on her own. I stayed in touch by phone and internet and

Skype. The NIH generously subsidized her travel from Dallas to DC, including long shuttle bus rides from Reagan or BWI airport. We had reached an impasse. There was no way forward with the sirolimus alone. She was dying slowly but surely. The doctors could see it—their eyes gave it away—and now I could see it too.

Elizabeth would have a room at the NIH during this important visit, and I stayed at a hotel in Bethesda used by the family and spouses of patients. Some other patients would also stay there, depending on the severity of their condition and their place in the LAM queue and the other diseases being treated at the NIH.

I remember many things about that stay, my first one, but one thing stayed with me. After breakfast at the hotel, the usual fare for basic hotels, we would await the shuttle that took us to the NIH, a couple of miles away. Patients, family, and loved ones. Oxygen tanks, respiration devices of several kinds, wheelchairs, walkers, crutches. "The halt and the lame."

I will remember as long as I live the generosity and the patience they showed toward each other. When the kindly driver pulled the shuttle bus up, he would get out and open the doors and put down a footstool and generally offer his aid. All the contraptions notwithstanding, people would offer, "No, you go first" or "I'll get back there" or "Let me help you" or "Do you have room enough for that?" Disease, the great leveler, can also be the entry into a new land of kindness and a curious form of strength and attentiveness. Slowed down by disease and illness, time slowed, you saw people's eyes and their looks of concern and their smiles of understanding and care and compassion. We are all in it together. What is health but this?

That was probably a good threshold to be going through, for things ahead were going to be hard, as it would turn out. This was the first time I sat across the desk or ward or hospital room with doctors and researchers whose names were now household words, people Elizabeth had gotten to know intimately over four long years of close association and care; but not me, until now. The question was the state of deterioration over such a long time. The draining system had been a mixed blessing, as noted, but it had also scarred the lung bottom. We were now looking at a badly damaged set of lungs, which had fought as hard as they could and were tired and losing this summoned strength.

The question before us was whether to do a pleurodesis procedure, given all the problems that it might lead to, if in the end a transplant became necessary. Several days' worth of tests were in order.

The LAM team working with Elizabeth, it should be underscored, were the world's premier physicians, surgeons, and researchers dedicated to treating LAM and discovering its root causes so that it could be stopped.

I would come and go from the hotel and stay as long as possible during the day. A friend of mine, a former student from my Yale teaching days, was now an Episcopal priest in the area. He came to visit and to offer prayers and support. We were coming to a critical moment of reckoning. He sensed that.

When all the tests and X-rays and consultations among the experts were completed, we gathered in Elizabeth's small hospital room. The newcomer in the group was the surgeon himself, who would be called upon to do a pleurodesis should it come to that next stage. There was something about the somber mood that was almost palpable, as we gathered that day. I can feel it even now. No one wants a pleurodesis, and so almost any news was going to be a tough pill to swallow. It is risky and difficult. It is band-aiding a problem to extend life. LAM isn't disappearing because of it but hiding around its edges as the lung is artificially attached by scarring to the lung wall, since it can no longer function as it should. You can't drive on a patched tire and pretend it's a properly functioning onc.

The news we received was not what I was expecting, I will confess. They would not do a pleurodesis. We had, of course, been praying that by some good fortune or godly intervention the lungs were going to rebound, due to the success of the LAM medication over this time.

Perhaps with the tube system gone, the lungs had begun to repair themselves.

But the news was not this and the faces of the team signaled the sober truth. The lungs were too damaged to even consider a surgical intervention in the form of a pleurodesis. They could not be made to attach to the lung wall. They were just too far gone. Surgeons do what they do in circumstances that defy reality and so are toughened and are prepared to get cutting and stitching and to look strong and sure, as well we might hope they would. To see such a wise head shake and such sure hands fold and collapse at the side is a weighty thing, a defeat that is hard to admit but which is the truth of the matter all the same.

You flounder a bit at times like this, facing such a terrible truth. Are you *sure*? Are there *no* other options? If it were your own sister or wife, what would you counsel? But you could see that the team knew this is where the journey was ending. There were no other paths, no secret vaults with special tonics, no higher specialists to call in, no new books to consult, and no new procedures to weigh.

The surgeon summoned some brave words. His mother had cancer. All she did, he said, was focus on it, dwell on it, let it rule her life. "Don't do that," he said.

"How far can you walk? Can you walk a hundred yards?" Yes. "Two hundred?" Yes. "How about a mile?" Yes, with some difficulty, but yes. "I suggest you do what you want to do with your life, and not let this rule you. Take advantage of the strength and health you do have. The sirolimus will continue to be prescribed. If it comes to the point where there is nothing more to do, and you cannot walk even across the room, there is always the possibility of a lung transplant, should that be possible. That day is not now. Do what brings you joy. We have done all we can."

The only real comfort I took away from that was that every door had been tried, and that the first string was on the field, and that we were not turning down a hard option. There were no more options to choose or doors to open. Four years down the road, from September 2011 to August 2015, we were now on a path without any markers or guardrails.

4

"Live Your Life." Off to France

LEAVING

As a bit of background, I should say that I have spent a lot of my life in Europe. Growing up with a name like "Seitz" and with a grandfather especially tuned into relatives and ancestors in Germany created in me a sense of belonging to the past and to another place. Living in rectories provided by churches for my family also made me long for a "home" of my own.

When I was in college, I worked for a company out of Boston that conducted six-week VW bus tours across Europe. One of my first stops was to see my German relatives in Schwetzingen, a charming village on the outskirts of Heidelberg. On those tours—six weeks in two VW buses with twelve teenagers—we saw London, Salisbury, Stratford, Oxford, Paris, Loire Valley, Pyrenees, Pamploma, Madrid, Barcelona, Carcassonne, the Riviera, Pisa, Rome, Florence, Salzburg, Vienna, Prague, Regensburg, Munich, the Rhine by boat, Amsterdam, and all the countryside in between. We climbed the highest mountain in Austria, kayaked on the Danube, biked the Dutch countryside, ran with the bulls in Pamplona, and hiked and camped on lovely estates and homes. We handed out Kennedy dollars as a small thanks to kind hosts who allowed us to pitch our tents on their land.

After enrolling at Yale for graduate studies, I attended Goethe Institute in Munich and decided to stay put. The University of Munich hosted me and encouraged me to pursue doctoral studies there. I made lots of friends, learned the language, and stomped all over Munich in the way one gets to know a place without a car. After I was ordained, I would return in the summers and take services for the Anglican vicar holidaying in Norway, staying in the church lodgings provided for him and his wife. Theology is a discipline deeply rooted and highly developed at the ancient universities of Heidelberg, Tübingen, Marburg, and "newer" schools in Göttingen, Munich, Bonn, and dozens of other locations. I visited and lectured at several of these once my professional profile was on the radar screen. I was awarded a prestigious Alexander von Humboldt Fellowship and spent a year in Munich writing a commentary on Isaiah, sponsored by my former tutor from years before.

In the late 90s I left my tenured post at Yale to accept a chair at the University of St. Andrews, Scotland, in love with these ancient centers of learning. I lived there for nine years before returning to North America. I enjoyed the proximity to the European continent and visited often during those years. I explored Scotland top to bottom and side to side, wandering down single-track roads, boarding ferries, climbing Ben Nevis, the Goatfell of Arran, and the remote Bienn an Or on Jura, driving the "long and winding road" down to Campbeltown. I played more than a hundred golf courses, my favorites often with only an honesty box for five quid a round and electrified lines to keep the sheep off the greens. I visited the graves of my mother's McConnahaugh relatives and had a kilt of her clan made, the Scottish equivalent of formal dress wear. Horseback riding and Scottish dancing were baked into the system in rural Fife. At times I could look about, especially in the forests of the Cairngorms, and see the regions of my birth and upbringing in western North Carolina, the Scots Irish home of American bagpiping, whiskey, kilts, and even highland games. No wonder they settled there.

So, when we left the NIH and considered our future, France seemed both a bold thing but also a very natural next step. We consulted with the NIH and determined there were LAM experts in Paris. Indeed, these dedicated laborers for health know each other well, are on a first-name basis, and have shared research and personal histories.

Elizabeth's business, French Affaires, was doing well and was a good thing for her spiritually and emotionally to be busy with during this ordeal. France has its own healing rhythms and sensibility. Shuttling between Toronto, Dallas, and France was a balancing act and a challenge. Taking Dallas out of the picture as our home base could simplify things a bit, even as it would remain Elizabeth's business base. I was approaching the time to begin thinking about how to do retirement, and France and a return to the Carolinas were contenders. And they didn't need to be hard alternatives for they might follow one another.

I had gotten to know the Church of England's Diocese in Europe through previous visits and had worked in Munich at the American Episcopal Church's version of that. We had spent a summer taking services in Bordeaux and the Medoc. A parish in Fontainebleau needed a one-third-time chaplain and we had visited the small congregation. I was interviewed by a small team, and I discussed the post with the bishop based in London. Part-time can become full-time without any effort, and parishioners constrained by budgets may accept the idea and then hope for more. I have a busy academic schedule so must guard my time carefully and knew already the challenges of that from previous such appointments.

They called me and I accepted. We would sell our Dallas house and rent a property in the area around Fontainebleau. Elizabeth had served as an *aide de famille* for a couple based in Paris in her earlier years and they had a second home near Fontainebleau. We attended the wedding of their daughter in the summer of 2015—the now grown-up woman whom Elizabeth had helped raise years ago. So, the region was familiar. Being less than an hour from Paris appealed. The specialists were based on the south side of Paris and not far by car.

Our house sale went so well and so quickly the agent never bothered to advertise. Now the questions of where to settle in France and the long list of things necessary to do that were on our plate.

Elizabeth had taken the Dallas Garden Club on a glorious trip to see the gardens and chateaux in Paris and down into the Loire Valley, in May of 2015. You may know Vaux-le-Vicomte north of Fontainebleau and of course the historical residence of the kings of France and then Napoleon himself in Fontainebleau proper. Vaux-le-Vicomte is breathtaking, and it has a rival, for different reasons, in the small town of Courances, about twenty minutes west of Fontainebleau. The chateau of Courances is a seventeenth-century estate renowned for its water gardens and forest tracks. I had enjoyed seeing the photos of the Garden Club visit there, en route to Amboise and the well-known Loire Valley chateaux. Grand, simple, uncluttered, unfussy. The word "Courances" is not clearly related to but otherwise exemplifies the verb "to run," as in running, coursing water.

The general region is full of deep underground water sources. Every house in Courances had its own well and running water was not plumbed into houses until 1957, so bountiful and accessible was and is the water.

St. Blaise des Simples is one of the many patron saints of the region, which because of the water also teemed with medicinal plants and herbs. He treated those infected with leprosy returning from the Crusades. The parish church of Courances is named for St. Stephen, the first Christian martyr, a physician by reputation and the patron of healing ministry down through the ages. A fact that at the time we did not know but that proved in time auspicious indeed.

The Marquis and Marquise of the chateau, and their wider family, own several rental properties in the village of Courances and in the nearby village of Fleury-en-Biere. The Marquis, now deceased, survived by his widow in her nineties and often resident in the chateau, had been the mayor of the village for fifty years. He had exchanged one of his holdings next to the school for the Catholic *presbytère*, or rectory, next to the twelfth-century parish church of St. Stephen (St Etienne). It was one of those in-house deals famous in its day, but was done in good spirit, to encourage the tiny school and offer it hope of years to come. Villages like Courances have typically lost their *maternelle* or nursery/kindergarten schools. The Marquis sensed that danger and so also set aside a parcel of land for the development of new housing, so families could afford to live in the village and raise their kids there, walking them by hand every morning, noon, and then afternoon back and forth from home to school to home.

Elizabeth knew the *gérant* or administrator of the chateau from trips she had taken there. He knew we were considering a possible home in France and then learned of my coming to the Anglican church in Fontainebleau. The tenant in the *presbytère* was shortly to leave. Might we be interested in renting it for our home in France?

Elizabeth had taken a drive-by look during one of her trips, from Paris to southwest France, and then I visited after her, during my Fontainebleau interview. It certainly had all the right signatures: a rectory suitable for the new Anglican chaplain, but in a stunning mediaeval village set apart, and healing herbs and water bubbling up from God's abundance in the Department of Essonne. It would need work, but it had good "bones," as Elizabeth would say. The chateau knew this work was necessary and agreed to undertake it, overseen by the thorough and well-organized *gérant* Patrick, who would become our friend and colleague.

We had several months to pack up the house and organize the move. I had crossed the Atlantic with furniture before when I moved to Scotland. You never quite get used to watching all the goods carefully packed in the sea containers, and this time we were taking a car as well. They put that in last. It takes a skinny mover to do it, or you'd have to go out through the sunroof.

The actual details for the visa were handled by the consulate in Houston. Big packets of papers would become go-to files over the coming years. Marriage, birth, bank account, work contract, and the list goes on, with photos, original copies and duplicates, passports, health statements, and so on. You get an appointment, drive to Houston, sit in a tiny piece of France in Texas, and do the necessaries, hoping for a kindly *fonctionnaire*. We got one. It was relatively painless.

Our goods gone, our house empty, a rented storage unit packed to the gills, we said our final goodbyes and handed the keys to the happy new owners. There is always something surreal and frightening about these moments, stripped of the daily orientating goods and routines, and alone before the journey to a new home. We got a ride to the airport reminding ourselves that Dallas was not disappearing, and our things would be with us in a new home after their journey across the North Atlantic.

ARRIVING

The flight from DFW to CDG isn't an old shoe but we do know it well, and as we arrived the paths to customs and bags and rental car were familiar ones. Our papers were all in order and our bags were there on the carousel ready to be hauled to Hertz. We would rent a car for several weeks to allow time to buy a new car locally. It was dark but becoming clear and bright, a December day in northern France. Paris sits on the same latitude as northern North Dakota and would have the same weather were it not for the warming currents of the Gulf Stream.

It takes about ninety minutes from Roissy, as the airport northeast of Paris is known, to the tiny rural village of Courances, depending on the fickle Paris traffic, the direction, and the time of day.

The chateau had contracted the renovation of several farm and work shed outbuildings, including the original water-wheel mill. These would be managed by Pierres d'Histoire (stones of history), a business devoted to short-term rents in historical settings. At the chateau of Courances, three had been just completed—the Mill, the Atelier, and the Pump—each outfitted with tasteful furnishings, nicely stocked kitchens, wood-burning fireplaces, TV, Wi-Fi, and stacks of wood at the door. If one wanted to rent all three, there were connecting doors, a feature that Elizabeth would plan to take advantage of with her popular French Cookbook Club groups from Dallas. Our home for a month would be the Mill, nicely cozy due to the sound of the passing water and turning wheel. Our future home was but a hundred meters away and would be a work zone during this time as it was prepped, sanded, painted, outfitted with a new kitchen, had sisal carpets laid, fireplaces cleaned, chimneys swept, and was generally cleaned up into a nice ancient shine.

Patrick had kindly put on the heat and stocked the kitchen with things to get us going. Milk, coffee, tea, some local jam, and of course a nice bottle of wine. It fell to me to begin what would be my almost daily routine: the walk to the boulangerie for fresh croissants and baguettes, still warm from the oven. We were the fortunate small village that had been able to attract and keep a bakery, these small shops typically run by a couple, rising early and working hard, proud of their wares, and source of local gossip. Sign boards tell of piano lessons, dog sitting, upcoming events, buying a quarter cow from the local farm, or fresh cheese and milk and yoghurt. Handymen of various description.

It would in time include announcements of a special Christmas service with carols in English and French, which I and the local Catholic priest together organized for the village, full of holiday family and friends from the world over. The chateau owners in full array—the Marquis, brothers and sisters in the next generation, children, and grandchildren—would be present at this time of year, and the municipal and chateau hunts well under way in the vast forest tracks that surrounded us on all sides. Christmas had just come and gone, and so the spirit of all that was still hanging in the air when we arrived. Brightly wrapped boxes simulating real presents festooned the school and *Mairie* I passed on return to the Mill. Coffee on and bread ready to be slathered with fresh butter and jam. Jet lag somehow feels better on a full stomach.

It would be several weeks before I could start my work at St. Luke's Fontainebleau. This is due to the new and extremely tight protocols for safeguarding. Even when I had my FBI materials in hand, they had to be physically in the possession of Church of England safeguarding officials in London. I have worked in the UK and Canada, in addition to the US, and the FBI counterparts in those countries are also meant to provide clearance.

In a way this was fine with us. We had plenty to keep us busy. Waiting for our furniture and car to arrive, picking out all the things necessary for the renovation of *le Presbytère*, finding the best places to shop for food, buying a second car in France, new cellphone and cable contracts, and especially getting our healthcare in order. Some of this had to wait on my actual start date at the church, but much of it could be initiated. For those of you familiar with French bureaucracy, better to get cracking early. The cul de sacs and dead falls will reveal themselves as one starts down the road.

As such things go, it turned out not to be too bad. Chest X-rays at the health center for the Essonne department, a check-up, medical history, questions to answer. Obviously, Elizabeth's lungs were hiding nothing from an X-ray machine, and we were prepared for that. We had her files and a letter from the French LAM specialist. The obvious worry was pre-existing conditions and how that would be handled. Here the connection to the NIH and their international partners in France helped enormously. Elizabeth is a research patient and would be under the care of the specialist team in Paris. None of this concerned the doctors doing this screening for basic healthcare. We found them professional, kind, and even good-humored.

The basic healthcare in France is superb. It covers all healthcare matters, including pharmacy care and medicines. Our doctor was recommended to us—a committed Anglophone in love with the US—and his office is in our market town of Milly la Fôret. French doctors still do house calls. Nurses come by in their own cars to do the kinds of things Elizabeth would need at home. We would get to know their kids, families, pets, lives. Healthcare has a homey feel, reminding me of the 50s and the physician with the bag and the office in his home. Yet it is also high caliber in the land of the first surgical theatres and medical schools able to do postmortem research when that was regarded as macabre and immoral.

LIVING

Off to a solid start with the chores of relocation, we were enjoying the freedom to see churches in the area before my post started up. My appointment was directly from the bishop so we would not worship at St. Luke's in Fontainebleau until the actual start date, though we were able to visit parishioners and get to know the parish informally. This was a fun time for Elizabeth to locate *brocante* dealers and search for furniture suitable for our seventeenth-century house. Electronics are also a special challenge, as I recalled from my decade in the UK, due to the different current. Lamps, TVs, radios, appliances there all needed to handle the 220 voltage, as you would instantly fry to a crisp any AC device brought from the US. I found a nice used VW station wagon that would in time be the traveling home of the dog we wanted to add to our French home and life.

We were living in the rectory of the Catholic church in Courances, with which we shared a wall and booming steeple bells.

To describe our life, it would be necessary to say a word about the Catholic church in France, since it leaves its imprint even today on daily life in villages like ours. The history of church and state in France is complicated, going back to the Reformation, the Revolution, the legal separation of church and state in 1905, and wars of religion prior to that, not to mention the Avignon papacy itself. As it impacts our village, the story is straightforward.

Church property, including rectories and parish halls, were given over to the civil communes at the beginning of the twentieth century. Even secular French citizens would be reluctant to see churches fall into ruin or disrepair and the idea of pulling down the enormous crucifixes at the entrance to towns is unthinkable. This is the French pride in *patrimoine.* It was until recently illegal to name children willy-nilly, and not all that long ago when saints names would be the logical choice in conjunction with the given birthday. The postal service, to raise a bit of money, or local *sappeur pompier* (fire brigade) sell you calendars for the new year in late November, with each day bearing the name of a saint. So, the border between church and state is both legally in place and culturally porous.

Attendance at funeral masses is almost *obligatoire.* The notices are posted by the mayor and may be seen in the tiny boulangerie. Our mayor, a lovely Portuguese woman, is in the front row at Mass when services are held in our church.

The best part of the arrangement between church and state is that the state is charged with maintaining all the church property, and in most regions of France does so with pride. We were having lunch with the priest in the parish nearest to us when a well-known tradesman entered and they exchanged happy pleasantries. The priest explained afterward to us that "Pierre" worked for the mayor's office and in that capacity did all the handy-man chores that cropped up at the rectory where he lived.

The man would likely never go to Mass—we did not recognize him—but he clearly respected and even loved our aging Père. When we happened to be in the butcher or baker or wine shop and "mon Père" was there, he clearly used the opportunity to show goodwill and a welcoming spirit. Yet visits to schools were another matter, and wearing religious garb (clerical collar) would have been forbidden. Even if school kids attended Mass regularly, it would not follow that one could ask the teachers to let them practice Christmas carols so they could attend and help with singing at a Christmas Eve service. That would be crossing a line, even though one might receive the news with a wry smile or a sympathetic brow. C'est La France.

More could be said, but for the purpose of our story it is important to note the warmth and bonhomie that we felt as non–Roman Catholic Christians, at least in our small village, and with their knowledge that I was a priest/minister/pastor/chaplain of some description and so to be ranged in some way alongside our friendly Père. The Catholic parish family we would get to know very well in the months and years to come, and their support and compassion and prayers were a lifeline, and are so still. Elizabeth and I would find ourselves dependent upon and buoyed along by the kindness and steady support of this doughty body of Christians.

Elizabeth was remaining busy with her French Affaires work. Several good reasons account for this. It is a project that excites her and that she loves. As the surgeon at NIH counseled: Do not let LAM rule your life and dominate your thoughts. Well and good, but thoughts must go somewhere and for her this was her life in, and love affair with, France. Second, it was a project taking off. The fact that we now had a home in France increased the appeal and cachet, especially at so charming a locale as 7 Rue du Petit Paris, Courances, next to a gorgeous chateau property, to which we, as renters, had access. And finally, she did not want people to know about her illness. She wanted to send the signal, "full steam ahead." *Joie de vivre* drops down a notch when it must sit alongside *l'epreuve de maladie*. We were also anxious not to have LAM disease become a topic of common knowledge in our new church family in Fontainebleau. It is not the easiest of diseases to explain or understand, and it was also at that point an ailment not visible to the public eye. We wanted to live our life as best we could and not call attention to ourselves.

We loved our life in the Mill and had set up shop there while work on our house pressed on. It was wise to let the workmen take their time and put things in great shape for our moving in. We wanted to time this, moreover, in conjunction with the arrival of our goods in le Havre. The moving company had a way to track the progress of the massive container ship, which after leaving Houston and crossing the North Atlantic went first to German ports before making its way back west to Rotterdam and finally our own destination. Of course there could be smaller tasks to complete, but if carpet was laid upstairs, everything painted, kitchen installed, we could accommodate the arrival of our furniture and begin, after about a month in the Mill, to take up residence and feel at home at last.

The driver and the workmen arrived from Normandy as scheduled and things began to emerge again from the container. First the car came out, and we stored it in a nice temporary place until we could get around to having it examined and cleared for driving in France. The Texas plates certainly let neighbors know we were here for real and not just vacationing. The unloading went as these things go, and after several hours we had what felt like a good start on our new life. Over the coming weeks and months Dallas things would be joined by French things, including nice antiques we had been identifying at local *brocante* stores and antiquity shops in our area. *Le Presbytère* at 7 Rue du Petit Paris was becoming our new home at long last. Fires roared in the fireplaces, meals were prepared in our new kitchen, cable TV brought local stations as well as international favorites. Internet life connecting us to Toronto and Dallas and friends across the world was tinkered with and recalibrated and humming along as routines returned to normal now in the village life of Courances, fifty kilometers south of Paris in the forest of Fontainebleau.

5

Heartache

As we were moved in and were becoming more at home in our locale, with its shops, churches, bookstores, service stations, hardware stores, post offices, and pharmacies, Elizabeth was readying herself to fly back across the Atlantic to Dallas for French Affaires work. She would have fun stories to tell of our new life as she took up older rhythms of language teaching, cookbook club, lecturing, FA promotional events, and seeing friends and clients. Taking advantage of being in the US, she had scheduled a visit to the NIH for a routine check-up.

What they discovered was not good news and dampened our enthusiasm at having a new life in France to dive into, for its own sake and as a welcome diversion from the realities of LAM. The tests they do to evaluate her lung effectiveness showed a sharp drop in their health and working capacity. A two-day stay would become a two-week period of evaluation and diagnosis. What we were learning about was not unexpected for the doctors tracking the path of LAM, though its exact timetable is not easy to predict or discern. After more than four years of struggling with LAM assault, her lungs were functioning even less well. This brings the patient to the next reality to be faced. Without lung power sufficient to provide needed oxygen to heart and organs, hypertension results. The heart is not getting enough octane to do its work properly, and it enlarges and overworks in an effort to do its job. Pulmonary hypertension is the name for this development, and it is experienced by advanced LAM patients suffering from the disease.

So now we were about to enter the terrain of manifest LAM deterioration. Elizabeth would need assistance to breathe. Hourly monitoring of oxygenation, and more, with the device one puts on the index finger and awaits its red-letter verdict, would be the new norm. Tubes and a portable respirator would be the new daily attire. At first it would be possible to leave it behind for public events to maintain privacy and a modicum of life as usual, but not for very long times and not for many more months to come.

It was good to have her back home even as the news was hard. You can't cheer these trials and hardships away. Elizabeth is a beautiful woman, inside and out. The thought of being harnessed to a respirator did not come easily. Even harder was the knowledge that things were going downhill and they would never get better now. Even a short respite from the breathing machine help was but for a season. The machine was keeping her alive by protecting her heart and her organs, and it would not be long before it was a necessity 24/7, day and night.

I had been on a search for a breeding kennel for a special French dog I wanted to bring into our life for many months now, ever since I had spotted the breed in a café in Fontainebleau in the summer of 2015. A Braque d'Auvergne. We were having a long lunch outside when a proud owner emerged with a sturdy hunting dog with a strong jet-black head. Could I ask the breed? Temperament? Good responses from the owner backed up by the handsome dog welcoming our caresses. I had previously raised a Weimaraner and liked the size and strength of the breed, but they can be demanding. The Braque d'Auvergne is a dog powerful, athletic, sensitive, and kind in equal measures. So, I have learned through my studies and so would prove to be true.

I felt instinctively that a dog would be a good companion in France and especially in our country location. But I also felt strongly that he would be a help to Elizabeth and to me in the coming trials. For all kinds of reasons. Dogs have a purpose in life, and it is to do all they can to love their owners and seek the welfare of the people who care for them. That may sound romantic and certainly it need not be so. But I am of the view that the right breed with the right love and training will give its life quite literally for its owners. We needed that and were prepared to do our part.

The kennel we found online was in the Ariège about an hour south of Toulouse. There are several main north–south autoroutes that one can access from Courances. One goes to Bordeaux, one to Toulouse via Limoges, Brive, and Cahors, and the *autoroute du soleil* to Aix and the Riviera.

The Braque d'Auvergne is a French pointing dog, perfected around upland game birds that thrive in France, like pheasants, partridge, quail, what we call chukkers in North America, and of course any game bird more generally, ducks included. "Braque" is an old French word meaning to point. "d'Auvergne" is the region in Central France, the central massif range of mountains, replete with dormant volcanoes. It lies to the north-east of the Midi region (Toulouse), and shares something of the same far-flung flair.

In France there are other breeds of Braque, pointing dogs, belonging to the general class of *chien de chasse*, hunting dog. *Braque francaise* and *Braque de pyrenees* are lesser known and rarer. German distant cousins are German short-haired pointers, popular for hunting in the US and in France as well, and the stylish but demanding Weimaraner. The English pointer is regarded as the toughest and hardest working pointer, but don't get into an argument about that at the RABA gatherings and field trial events (*réunion des amateurs de Braque d'Auvergne*). Dogs like this are also called *chien d'arrêt*, for their job is to find game that typically broods and then runs away when sensing danger, and to make them stop. Hard-wired into their sturdy and committed hunting instinct is the signal that they have found what they and their owners are looking for: game now frozen and hiding in thick brush. Thereupon they hold their frame firmly and raise the fore-hock of right or left leg.

Get ready.

A young Braque, as we would learn, will chase anything that flies. Butterflies, non-game birds, insects, bees (watch out), and even the shadows all these cast on the ground.

Internet sites can give you lots of information but there is always the possibility of inflated and misrepresented truth on the ground. The breeding kennel Ruisseau de Montbrun, by contrast, was just exactly as "on the tin." We had made an appointment and arrived just a bit late, due to tricky roads and befuddled GPS signals. Montbrun is a local stream, and the location of the kennel was not in a village per se but in what the French call a *hameau*. The owner, Madame S., with whom we had been communicating by internet and phone, greeted us. Proud of her work and rightly so, she led us to one of several small concrete kennel facilities, set up perfectly for birthing and whelping, with a little sanctuary so mom could withdraw for a needed breather. Nine pups is a lot of work.

There she was resting, and there was the huddled clump of nine squiggly babies doing their puppy thing of growing day by day. Getting to know the big world of themselves and each other and the visitors from a bigger world they would one day enter and make their own, on their own. For now it was the daily fun of squirming, eating, pooping, establishing rank, and doing it all over again and again.

It was not too difficult to find the ones we narrowed our choice down to. Madame held them up for us to view, as we were to keep our germy distance. After a thorough review of the males—we wanted a boy dog—we returned to the two that we thought were our finalists. Madame's eye was trained to know each one and to record our choices, helped by collars of different hues.

"M" seemed a difficult year to be born for naming. We wanted a French name, and the two that resonated with us were Marcel and Marius, the latter a popular old Provençal name and the former the name of a favorite Provençal author and movie director, Marcel Pagnol. We loved his stories and his films, so Marcel would be his name.

These are especially fond memories, and they remain fresh to this day. I suspect some of that is that the coming months would get messy and hard. The little *chambre d'hôte* and puppies at Ruisseau de Montbrun offered a charming respite and helped us forget the struggles at hand. Shortly I would take up the routines of St. Luke's Fontainebleau and affairs in the Diocese in Europe. I was soon to be off to Brittany for the annual Synod of France weekend retreat and meeting, where bishop, parish clergy, and representatives gathered for conducting business and hearing lectures and presentations of various kinds.

The idea of a Diocese in Europe for the Church of England is a bit odd, but it has a rather long history. The details of that do not need detain us. The Diocese is the largest geographically in all the thirty-eight Provinces of the worldwide Anglican Communion, numbering around eighty million Christians. It stretches from Russia to Gibraltar, from Norway to Malta. The largest collection of churches is in France, due to the large number of expats spread across the lovely French countryside. You'd have a second home in France or seek employment there for the weather alone, leaving aside the style of life, wine, and super cuisine. NATO had been in Fontainebleau and there is a strong international school there and a fine business school linked with Wharton in the US and with a second campus in Singapore, called INSEAD. Multiply that reality, if for different reasons, across the length and breadth of France, and especially popular areas for the British like the Dordogne. Hence there are over sixty Anglican parish churches in France alone.

The annual clergy gathering in 2016 was held at the Catholic monastery/retreat center of St. Jacut, a little beyond St. Malo, on the north coast of Brittany. Early spring brought decent weather for walking the severe low tide beaches of Bretagne. It was a good outing for getting a feel for the diocese and the many clergy and parishes stretching from Pas de Calais to Pau, from Nantes to Alsace. Many were part-time posts like mine, but others larger and more stable numerically.

On the last day an announcement was made at lunch concerning an evening event exclusively dealing with clergy healthcare. This came as a bit of a surprise as we had organized our healthcare pretty much on our own, and through a standard plan unrelated to the church. I went along and discovered that all clergy in France are to be rostered in a special healthcare dedicated to that vocation and subsidized accordingly by the parishes where one was posted. The plan we were already enrolled in was not expensive, but it was also not one the parish played any financial role in. It was also clear that this other health plan, called CAVIMAC, was a mandatory benefit and all parishes were required to enroll their clergy in it. France and the Diocese in Europe both expected compliance with this.

It was unclear why St. Luke's had not done this. The explanations offered did not square with the counsel we sought and were given by the Anglican priest in Maisons Allfort charged with representing clergy for CAVIMAC coverage. Elizabeth was on a respirator 24/7, she needed steady and reliable healthcare given what she was facing now, and all the medications prescribed for her deteriorating condition. The problem was a complicated one. If we left the coverage we had (healthcare A) for a coverage we were supposed to have at CAVIMAC (healthcare B), what if we encountered problems in the transition? Why had the parish not enrolled us, as the contract upon review clearly stipulated they were to do? Shades of our earlier healthcare problems in Dallas started to haunt us.

After all the disturbing dust had settled, we successfully transition to CAVIMAC and the parish began undertaking the required co-pays. But none of this sat well with us. The problems of pulmonary hypertension were increasing day by day. The respiratory machine's dial was going in a direction that told the tale, and it would become increasingly difficult to stray long from its necessary assistance.

6

Crisis

ELIZABETH HAD BEEN MEETING with the specialist in Paris, Dr. Marc Humbert, and in April we were scheduled to go up together. Dr. Humbert spoke excellent English. And we were becoming fluent in the French language version of what was going on, in the orbit of technical discussion a disease like this rotates in. God had provided in Dr. Humbert, one of the world's experts, not only in LAM disease but also quite specifically in pulmonary hypertension, his area of proven renown. His nurse showed us into his office. French specialists like this hold professorial chairs and indeed his manner was akin to that. The other way to put it is that in the US doctors are surrounded by the symbols of their hauterie and training. The facilities are typically shiny and give off the aura of what would have been the mediaeval cathedral of its day: powerful, staffed to the hilt, professionally busy, temples of science and the Latin glossaries bearing witness to their rarity and sophistication. That is also the case, in its own way, in France, but with none of the dress and shine. Modest facilities, modest care givers, modest stairwells and parking garages and restaurants, even a bit shabby. Money does not flow to these things but to the research itself and the specialist care that results from it. You get a sense of keen and penetrating intellect, content to speak for itself in that spare genre. In many ways it is much more reassuring because undisguised and candidly human. Face-to-face with the doctor you feel he isn't hiding anything. His manner says he knows what he is talking about and you should know what he is thinking straightforwardly and without art.

Elizabeth's heart would continue to struggle. The lungs were out of strength and had done all they could. The respiratory machine would struggle to keep up. Her heart would be taxed beyond its capability. Only a transplant could save her life in the end. And he assured us that this would happen and that it would save her life. He was in charge. The road was not unknown to him. He would do what was required. One day he would come to see her run again. Now, however, we would be on a marathon of a different kind and with a finish line of life, or death. All avenues of care had been exhausted.

As the summer months arrived, we knew we were in new and final territory. We arranged to pick up our little Marcel a bit north of Toulouse. We used the opportunity to stop in a breathtakingly beautiful village called Saint-Cirq-Lapopie, north of Cahors. Madame S. handed over our new bundle at a designated rest area and we headed back to our home in Courances. Marcel whined a bit but was otherwise sturdily adjusting to his new kennel cage and our VW station wagon. A few stops for bathroom breaks and we arrived late afternoon, tired from the quick to-and-fro journey. Marcel fell in love with the rich grass in our backyard. The bells were another thing. The Angelus consists of three triples and then a couple of minutes of steady tolling, and it sounds at 8 a.m., noon, and 5 p.m. He must be taken inside, or he will howl, a deep barking from an otherwise quiet and peaceful breed.

The diocesan bishop organized a special two-day orientation meeting at a retreat in Oxfordshire. It reminded me of how small Europe is, and instead of the trip from Edinburgh to continental ports of call, this was an even shorter flight from Orly to Heathrow. It was a useful set of sessions on all aspects of Church of England canon law and customs. The group consisted of new chaplains coming from other regions of Anglicanism outside of England, now taking up posts in Germany, Sweden, Italy, and two of us from France, myself and a Canadian at the parish in Marseille. I stocked up on strong cheddar cheese and returned.

Unfortunately, I contracted a low-grade pneumonia that festered until diagnosed a month later when I accepted it wasn't just a chest cold. Airplanes and close quarters are nice incubators.

But this was not good for Elizabeth. A case of pneumonia was dangerous, if not lethal. And sure enough I had infected her. She did not need this fresh challenge on top of everything else, and we were still unsure about the transition to a new healthcare plan.

In France ambulance services are privately run affairs. They are, of course, reimbursed by the healthcare system. One gets used to seeing their white vans with strong blue emblems indicating they are ambulance vehicles as one drives the roads in France. Consulting with her doctors we realized it was important to get her to the hospital as quickly as possible. The ambulance arrived. They disconnected her oxygen and connected her to their more robust system. It all was done at the gate of our courtyard, and she was reassured by efficient workers and then they set off.

This was starting to become more than she or I could take, this unfortunate and unnecessary turn of events. Marcel and I went inside and settled down. Unusually for our quiet residence at this time of day, the doorbell rang. I went to see who it was and opened the wooden gate to the smiling face of Père Mercier, the priest of the wider parish family, which included our church in Courances. He was just about to leave for the *grandes vacances* the French take for the entirety of August, returning to his family's home in the *Vendée*. He was just stopping by the parish church and thought he'd say hello before heading off.

The timing could not have been more auspicious. In my adequate but struggling French I explained what had happened. We did not then know each other well. He could sense my distress. I also explained priest to priest, friend to friend, the struggles with health insurance we were undergoing due to the negligence and insouciance at our Fontainebleau church. Knowing glances and shared frustration. Père Mercier can say little and say everything by his manner. I really needed just a few minutes and accepted that things were going to be fine. He pledged his prayers, and we would see each other again in September.

Elizabeth would remain in the hospital in Paris for two weeks as they stabilized her weak lungs and rid them of pneumonia. It was a shock, but she had got through it. The hospital would become a familiar place for her and us in the months to come.

We had scheduled a two-week vacation ourselves in Provence. We found a small gite where dogs were OK, just outside of Aix. There was a pool, which I was longing for. Dry air and sunny weather would be good for Elizabeth. It was a place we generally knew well, but also a new spot for us both, north of Pagnol country and at the foot of Mont Sainte-Victoire, outside a small town called Chateauneuf la Rouge in the *garrige* (scrubland) and vineyards characteristic of the region. Marcel could run free in their garden, so long as he looked out for their sizeable older male. Mont Sainte-Victoire is, of course, famous for the series of paintings done by Cézanne from his atelier home outside of Aix, during the years 1902–24. Now it was outside our little vacation home, if a good deal closer.

We had two pleasant weeks. The Olympics were on TV. Great restaurants to visit. A beautiful winding drive around the base of Mont Sainte-Victoire. Evening swims. Cookouts. Elizabeth's signature *salade niçoise en plein air*. Visits to Aix and down to our favorite village seaport, Cassis, with its stunning Calanques to visit via boat. Do not, however, contemplate a dip in the sea, at least not in July or August. No place for beach towel or car. Horrible traffic. We just turned around and went back to our gite retreat.

Fires are a constant threat this time of year. The forests are dry, the scrubland excellent tinder, and the winds stand ready to destroy huge tracks of land. So, you can't walk just anywhere and at any time. I wanted to hike on the numerous trails of Mont Sainte-Victoire and consider a trip to the top. In 1989, over twelve thousand acres or twenty square miles were ravaged by fire and the days on which you can venture on trails are very restricted. Marcel, Elizabeth, and I did a small walk one day, just to look at the signs and get a sense of the options.

I found a day free to hike and got to the top in under two hours. It rises over a thousand meters, and practically from sea level, so it offers a stunning profile and a challenging non-technical climb. At the top is a cross twelve meters high and a mediaeval chapel, as well as professional meteorologist stations and, of course, fire alert surveillance. Elizabeth and Marcel stayed at the base for obvious reasons and kindly waited for my return. The dry air and less inclining paths were still a good tonic for heart and soul.

With the coming of fall, the summer draws to a close. "After camp, there's laundry," a friend of mine would remark. But we were also aware of the falling of a final season. It would be time to return and start down the final leg of a journey ending now most likely in transplant, if we were so fortunate. One does not dial a transplant up or buy one online. There is a race between the disease and a lone donor's death that will give one life, or so it is hoped. You must go to the end, right up to the jaws of death, for there are others who need these precious organs, in straits just a bit more dire than your own. Elizabeth would soon be learning the ins and outs of a transplant surgery that would hope to give her life back to her. The shadow of death was drawing, in the form of a life-or-death shadow of preparation and waiting until the last moments of life, at the door of death itself.

We decided to leave a day or two early and drive back home. Home. A place of reality now setting in.

For us both there were assignments to complete and clutter to clear away. Life goes on, until it doesn't. I had to visit my PhD students in Toronto. I had agreed to give a series of public talks in Singapore, at the cathedral and at the Trinity Theological College there, and had completed the writing. I stayed a week there and returned, accompanied by their promises to pray for my wife.

Then there was St. Luke's, my one-third-time post in Fontainebleau. Lurking in small parishes like this are historical challenges with long tentacles, and getting at them in a fifteen-hour-a-week post is impossible. Yet they were festering and were coming, unsurprisingly, as they had done in previous decades, to the surface. We did not have the stamina or time to face into them properly. Fortunately, at long last our healthcare was in place and secure. We were advised by CAVIMAC, as well, that once one is enrolled, the care will not go away. Such is the concern of France for healthcare, even for those who have done the hard work to gain visas, annually. I conferred with the bishop and we said goodbye. Looking back now it was more than prudential. It would have been impossible to continue the Sunday routines and all the pastoral care emerging on the horizon. We would need to attend to the cares in front of us and on our very doorstep.

I want to speak personally at this point, for the trials of Elizabeth's condition were increasing. In October, at night, she was spooked by a spider in the bathroom, and trying to stomp it, broke her heel. A very, very painful bone to break. She could not walk, of course. At the emergency room in Melun a cast was carefully made. She would be confined to a wheelchair for the duration of the healing process. Respiration apparatus, wheelchair, crutches, how to get up and down the stairs, in and out of the car. It just seemed too much. I have a picture of us waiting in line in the freezing cold at the Prefecture of the Essonne Department, where we renewed our visas annually, fat file in her coated lap and head wrapped, shivering in the wheelchair as we waited our turn to enter the building.

Sickness has never been a friend or companion of mine. I hate it and am impatient with it when it strikes me. I have tried to ask why. I had three brothers. I went to a boy's boarding school for five years, from age thirteen to eighteen. We students did the manual labor, the days were regimented around work, sport, classes, chapel, study hall, with a single forty-five-minute period of free time before daily Evensong and dinner. Getting sick was not part of the regimentation. It would be not pulling one's weight—or worse, it would be a sign of weakness. Of course, we were in the prime of health and healthily active every day.

In addition, what there was of healthcare was a mixture of incompetent and perverse, let me say it bluntly. The doctor who came out once a week did so in part because it was fun to check for hernias in the most unlikely of cases, teenaged boys. We rolled with the punches, and it was a different era when boys stuck together and did not take this kind of thing too seriously. It was Dr. M., the nut job. The nurse in residence was nearly blind and, while harmless, clearly knew nothing about healthcare.

So, getting sick, if it happened, would be better endured in silence. It would pass.

But it is in my character as well to be single-minded. That's how books and journal articles get written and how tenure at Yale gets accomplished. Multi-tasking, Elizabeth will be quick to remind you about me, is an unknown characteristic. I was now stripping back my own work and having to focus on a health crisis. The "for worse, for poorer, in sickness, til death" side of the ledger was now the only register it seemed. I believe we both wanted a happy life after so much career and work, and we married with that expectation. What did we receive instead? Six years of a journey into disease and decline.

This would be a very hard season for me, in which I quickly had to get used to my obvious shortcomings and an adjustment to sickness and debilitation outside of my ken. Marcel was far more sensitive and caring. I was careening and trying simply to do my best, asking for a strength foreign to my ways and my past. If I was any good at all it would not be from my flesh unaided, but because of a commitment to care for Elizabeth and a strength not my own.

Then in January of the new year, my dad died. It happened quickly, in the course of a twenty-four hours, and even though he had been plagued with this and that ailment, it came as an unthinkable shock. Email is a terrible way to participate in a sudden and sharp decline and then the message, "He is gone."

You can conduct funeral services and sit at hospital beds with the sick and dying and even be relatively tuned in and moved with compassion. But one moves on, another death and funeral is around the pastoral bend. Death was now up close, seeping into my own mortal coil.

In the final chapter of Ecclesiastes, the preacher describes what sounds like the world coming to an end, or nature grinding to a halt, and as the Hebrew Bible specialist and modern commentator Michael Fox rightly notes, the world is indeed coming to an end. His own. Surveying the wreckage of the civil war, the death by fire of his wife, and the loss of his son, the American poet Henry Wadsworth Longfellow spoke of the hearthstones of a continent being rent. The line separating the outer world and the inner life was disappearing, as death and sickness had their way and rent a continent in two. Death was not out there. No, it was right here.

Elizabeth would spend these last fall months meeting with specialists at Marie Lannelongue Hospital in preparation for a transplant down the road. Preparation is multifaceted and takes many months of monitoring and readying and so would carry over into the spring. The road to Plessy Robinson, a leafy suburb south of Paris, would become well-worn. The medicine that had been keeping her alive would have to stop, as a condition for getting ready for a dramatic surgery. With the loss of this life-giving medicine her condition worsened considerably, but this is a necessary step, harsh though its effects are.

I flew over for my father's funeral and time with my mother and family. It was a good time, though hard. Upon return I did a week of intensive French in Tours, a week I'd had to reschedule. For obvious reasons it would be increasingly incumbent upon me to get better control of the French language. I had been working away at this for a year, but with Elizabeth's condition and our new life apart from expats speaking English, the language needed to improve. Our life was moving into France more resolutely. We were worshiping at the Catholic parish in Milly la Fôret, our friends were our village neighbors, Elizabeth's many French friends, and colleagues I was developing in Paris. We organized a Christmas Lessons and Carols Service, with hymns sung in French and English, with Père Mercier and me officiating. Despite tubes and wheelchair, Elizabeth produced a much-appreciated mulled wine. We were feeling at home. I participated in a conference on creation at the Catholic University of Paris/*Institut Catholique*, with professors from France, Germany, and the US. I was hoping to make some new professional connections in a new country of residence. But aside from the cultural realities of life in France, our attention would now turn to the transplant realities and the demands they would require of us.

7

The Cords of Death

ELIZABETH'S ACCOUNT OF THE months in the run-up to eventual transplantation would have given the intimate details of a struggle she alone would face, in a fight for her life. She never set aside the time to tell that story for reasons I do not know for sure. I accompanied her to Marie Lannelongue and sat beside her as we listened to this and that surgical team tell us what was going to be necessary. There were myriads of forms to sign. Housing for me in the area was discussed. Elizabeth met with psychiatrists. A documentary team asked if they could use her story.

The surgeons, nurses, and a specialist work in teams. You move from team to team. In time you meet with the one surgeon who will do what is routinely a twelve-hour transplant, joined by other surgeons to spell one another. The question was posed, obviously enough, was she sure, were we sure, France was the best place to face this dangerous surgical episode, or would we not want to return home?

That is a weighty question. But where is our home, we wondered? Our home in respect of LAM disease was the NIH in Bethesda, and the LAM specialists in France were all part of that same family. There were as well the obvious issues of how we would move back to the US, and where, and how we'd handle the health costs and the enlisting of surgeons.

It is important as well to speak of a fact governing organ transplant in France, though at the time it was not something we knew about. The topic arose when it came to signing forms giving the green light for the use of organs that had been kept alive artificially, or ones that had not been successful in keeping a patient alive but were still available for others in dire need next in line. We were asked to ponder that question at home, and in time we did agree. But what we learned in the context of this possible development was that in France a person must sign off not to have their organs available for transplant, instead of the opposite practice obtaining in the US and other countries. If you die in an automobile accident and have not expressly declared that your organs are not available, they are there to help save a life. And cars we had seen regularly marked *urgence* were ready to whisk the lungs to a nearby hospital or a waiting airplane, where they would be put to immediate, life-saving work.

Frankly, if we had any question about returning to the US, which we did not, this fact alone ruled in favor of our staying and putting her life in the hands of the experts putting their skills at our disposal. France takes its medical research with utmost seriousness and will take a backseat to no one when it comes to transplantation. Riding the elevators in Marie Lannelongue, one is impressed with this or that notice marking anniversaries of successful transplants, the first one done there not long at all after Dr. Christaan Barnard's first successful human-to-human heart transplant, done on December 3rd, 1967, at Groote Schurr Hospital in Capetown, South Africa. I can remember the event as being unbelievable for its day. Elizabeth would not have reached her third birthday at the time of this world-shaking achievement.

Marie Lannelongue, née Cibiel, after whom the hospital is named, was born in Rouen in 1893. She married at twenty-one the Viscount Pierre de Rémusat. She was widowed at twenty-five and devoted herself to good works, creating a free-of-charge school for girls in the Haute Garonne. During the war of 1870 (the Franco-Prussian war) she turned her home into a hospital for soldiers wounded in combat. There she met the brilliant surgeon Odilon Lannelongue, whom she married in 1876. He was from modest background, and she lovingly and enthusiastically funded his surgical career, propelling him to the height of French medicine. Two hospitals dedicated to heart and lung surgery resulted from this collaboration. The couple had no children. She died in Paris in 1906. The transplant hospital Elizabeth was to be operated on 111 years later in a quiet suburb of Paris was named in her honor.

It was a pleasant slowly warming spring in northern France. A friend from Toronto visited, and a bit later my brother, his first time in France. In March we had a final meeting with the lead surgeon. We'd had some bumpy discussions with several of the teams. There is the old joke about asking a surgeon to name the top three skilled professions: "You mean there are three?" You don't do this work without a strong will and overpowering confidence that you will be giving it your best. The lead surgeon was a bit older, and he bespoke the kind of quiet confidence and talent we needed. "We are going to make this happen," was his bottom line.

Marcel was scheduled to spend a month of training in le Perche, a couple of hours to the west of us, in upper Normandy, a region known for lakes and fishing and hunting in charming forest tracts. He was just old enough to start. The timing was pretty good. We needed to be ready. Elizabeth was to have a bag packed. The surgery was not immediate, but it was likely not far off. Without the sirolimus, her breathing went steadily down, and the oxygen requirement increased in the same measure. The dial on the machine could not go much higher. The oxygenation meter showed the steady decline. None of this is good on the organs. You lose your appetite. You lose, she lost, a lot of weight on a frame nowhere near heavy at any point in her life. Arms like thin sticks, pelvic bones sticking out, hard to bathe and do simple things. Confined to the couch. A terrible descent into hell. Nowhere to flee from the fact that day by day you are dying.

The time had long gone when we were able together to attend church. Even in a wheelchair and trailing respiration tubes, we so needed our time in church, with our parish support and friends, and the priests who followed affairs and dedicated their prayers and their ears, and the Lord God of mercy. From among the effects of my dad I had taken a pyx, the pocket watch looking instrument for taking the sacrament to the sick. I needed something of my dad at this time and anticipated its Sunday-to-Sunday use. I would leave it on the altar at the start of the Mass, and come forward at the close, with others also caring for sick relatives, and solemnly receive it for Elizabeth's home communion. A time often to cry and let go, supported now only by God's grace.

The time came in mid-May that Elizabeth's poor heart and lungs could not carry on anymore. A night bag and a midnight call that lungs were available would not be how this went. We called the ambulance, and they took her off to the specialists at Kremlin Bicêtre to a hospital room, for evaluation. Oxygen tanks had replaced the respirator's heroic best, and they were dialed all the way up and had been for some weeks. Her time had come.

As it happened Marcel's stay in le Perche was to end that same Friday and I had to go get him. I was hoping they could stabilize her condition, even as dire as it was, for a few days. I drove over and stopped at a church in le Croix du Perche to say a prayer and light a candle. I was in a village of less than a hundred and obviously a visitor. It just so happened that the church was open. A woman saw me praying and as I left asked where I was from. My French suggested I was not from le Perche, and I told her. She asked if she could say a prayer, and I said yes, that my wife was likely to soon undergo a lung transplant in Paris. Which hospital, she asked? It turned out she had been a nurse in Paris all her adult life and knew Marie Lannelongue very well. She is in good hands, she reassured me.

Small world. Big God.

The trainer put Marcel through his paces, and I thanked him, settled the bill and said I must be off. It was so good to see him and to have our family back together. I confess I needed him just now.

Elizabeth had been joined by a couple of Paris friends since I was going to be en route from an hour west. I had intended to drop Marcel off at home and speed up but thought I ought to call. Elizabeth was not doing well. I decided at once to drive straight to the hospital.

The situation was grave. I struggled to find her room, in the labyrinthine corridors and oddly conjoined wings, and exasperated, finally located her. Things were serious but her vitals were still stable. She was resting and would benefit from a quiet night. Frightened and concerned, but somewhat reassured, I headed home. Her friend Jane would stay with her for a short while and then head home.

No sooner had I arrived, and Marcel had a glimpse at his food and water bowls and back yard, than the cell phone buzzed. Jane was calling. Elizabeth was failing. They would take her to the transplant hospital right away and prep her for an operation that would require lungs we would now be waiting on. They put her number one on the urgent list. They were fighting to save her life.

I got in the car and sped up to Marie Lannelongue, going the right direction against the rush hour traffic heading out of Paris on a Friday afternoon. Fortunately, the gate attendant, whom I knew well by now, did not see Marcel in the back of the station wagon. I could not leave him. His Elizabeth needed him close by and waiting loyally.

Because of the rush hour and her grave state, they could not waste any time. Her heart was giving out. They could not force enough oxygen into her broken lungs anymore. They would need to oxygenate her system by exchanging her blood. The equipment for that was best hooked up in a room right next to the operating theater itself, a room from which she would leave only and if lungs were found and rushed to save her life. The helicopter was the only way to get her to this critical destination. Five minutes from Kremlin Bicêtre to Marie Lannelongue, counted off by one of the husky attendants who do this day in and day out, saving lives. She says he pointed out the Eiffel Tower as they zoomed past. She landed on the pad on the roof and was bustled down to the theater and prepped. We would be able to see her, we hoped, but were told it could be as late as midnight. We found couches in the waiting room and set about to wait for the call that we could go up and see her, for but several minutes we were told.

At last, the call came. We rode the elevator up, me going first, and were shown the room where you don the necessary sanitation costumes, including hats, boots, and facemasks. Her room was one she shared with others in the same condition as her, each with their own special and dedicated space, and monitored assiduously by a team of nurses at the center. A clear tube the size of a garden hose had been inserted into her left thigh, and the blood being oxygenated in this way was the last thing now keeping her alive. Point of no return. Every avenue tried. Every medicine used. Every machine hooked up. Every doctor and nurse doing all they could. Nearly six years of decline and suffering and exhaustion and now at final last stages more like death than life. But fighting and holding her own. The psalmist has expressed well Elizabeth's truth: "The pangs of death surrounded me . . . the snares of death confronted me, in my distress I called upon the Lord" (18:4–5).

I could squeeze her hand, kiss her cheek, tell her I loved her and would be back in the morning. At least I knew where she was, who was taking care of her, what that looked like, and how the routine of visiting her unrolled. "Love you, girl. I'll be back tomorrow."

I slept fitfully. Marcel was dead to the world. We would get the personal things together that a quick trip to the hospital via ambulance had not allowed. But of course, the space was highly controlled due to the threat of infection and all the patients there cleared of all medicines so the surgery could take place under proper conditions. A few framed pictures were OK. A small pine cross from our church in South Carolina that had been a companion along the way. A prayer book and Bible in French. I would take up things to read to her as we waited for lungs to arrive. How long would that take?

The odds we were told were good, though the measurements had to fit, so it was possible lungs would become available that were not suitable for Elizabeth's frame. But everything turned of course on her condition and how long she could last. She was close to death. No one was in doubt about that. They were keeping her alive by technology but it could not do everything alone and certainly not for long. A couple of weeks? Perhaps, at the very outset. Who knew whether these answers were aimed at keeping stamina up and hope alive.

Saturday and Sunday are the best days to drive to Paris from Courances. You can get to Marie Lannelongue in forty minutes if there are no accidents. The roads are clear, and the ride can be almost pleasant measured against the *embouteillage* (bottlenecks) so typical of a big city. The parking lot is clear and the hospital quiet. Staff is minimal, except of course in the urgent care units where Elizabeth was resident, where the dedicated nurses and doctors are on watch 24/7. The parking lot attendant saw Marcel and said dogs were not allowed, so we were busted. No problem. Lots of parking on the street right there. It would be his last visit. He could stay put in our yard during these days of urgent waiting and daily commuting.

I rode the elevator to the restricted floor and donned the outfit provided. They had lockers with keys for visitors. The woman in charge phoned in to be sure it was OK to enter. I now knew the route, down the hall to the last big hall on the left. Elizabeth was in the room closest to the surgical theatre, just across the corridor, or so I was told, as it was sealed tight to all but the surgeons and their teams.

Oxygen-assisted breathing throughout the larger space, patients recumbent and being kept alive by machines, the clicking and humming of monitoring machines, the shuffling sounds of nurse's booties and the quiet sotto voce briefing sessions with doctors. From time to time, they would poke in and speak with us, and answer questions or avoid them, depending on whether answers were possible or helpful. I do not know how they do their jobs. Talk about professional discipline. And when one patient leaves, another one is right behind to take their place. A lifetime of caregiving. Steady as she goes.

We weren't allowed to stay long. Elizabeth showed me her new oxygenation tube, better awake and composed now. She briefed me on the helicopter ride and last minutes at the hospital before being hustled off by life flight. We talked about her state of mind and concerns, of course. She knew this was the end of the line. No disguising that. There were only two mysteries left. How long she could live in this state, and when, and if, lungs would be found. We were trying to remain hopeful.

On Sunday I went to the earlier 9:30 service that takes place at one of the smaller village churches. The village of Moigny-sur-Ecole one could walk to in about thirty minutes, and I rode my bike there regularly for exercise. We'd hear their church bells, unless they were drowned out by our own. It is an especially beautiful church, having been recently renovated thanks to an ambitious and successful mayor's fund-raising campaign. It did not hurt that Nina Ricci and Christian Dior had in their day been resident in the quiet village. Tasteful and beautiful are their hallmarks. The church is stunning in simplicity and color and art. We attend the earlier services there and in Courances when the rotation enables that. The congregations are smaller, and we know our neighbors and regular worshipers.

How is Elizabeth? Each asked earnestly as we gathered for Mass, and I made my way up the aisle to my seat. Not good. Waiting now for a transplant. Ambulance to hospital, helicoptered to Marie Lannelongue. Need your prayers redoubled. We all missed her tubes and quiet dignity. Père Pascal, the lead priest in the three-person team was presiding and I sought him out to report the news. What a solid and reassuring presence. He would dedicate the Mass to petitions for Elizabeth. He knew it was grave, on death's door, no doubt from years of experience hearing reports like my own. In the course of the service, I found myself collapsing. Here I was in a tiny village in France, all alone, except for my wife whose life was France itself, and whose life was in mortal danger. If I lost her, where would I be?

Of course, I was surrounded by friends who had taken us into their lives and their homes. Some distinguished themselves by their courage, dedication to prayer, and support, going the extra mile about a disease easy to turn away from as hopeless and sad. But no. Concerned to buoy me up. Concerned that I carry on in my role. Offering the French phrase that sums it up best: *Bon courage*.

I took communion to Elizabeth later that Sunday. We prayed and asked God for a donor. We knew he was listening. It was harder to know his will on earth as it is in heaven, but we knew his only Son as well had experienced it all down here in the flesh. "For we have not a High Priest which cannot be touched with the feeling of our infirmities; but was in all points tempted like *as we are*, yet without sin" (Hebrews 4:15).

Months earlier, at my request, Père Mercier had provided me with a key to the church on our doorstep, whose sacristy door I could access from our own garden. It was my place of daily prayers, musty and cold but steady as a rock. It was now well worn with our kneeling.

You see things when your eyes are made to be opened, and adversity is a teacher harsh but certain to take us deeper if but by a grace outside us and our sense of strength. In the side chapel of the parish church next door there is the familiar painted depiction of the sacred heart of Jesus, above the altar.

His chest is opened onto a throbbing heart. In our painting his heart is encircled with thorns. Symbolizing, one supposes, his passion for us, those for whom he died. A heart of love and a heart that knows, that feels, our infirmities. Nothing we go through, he has not gone through ahead of us.

At a chapel in central France, at Saint-Haon-le-Chatel, I saw these words inscribed in a stone mantel:

Ou tu passes j'ai passé
Ou j'ai passé tu passeras
Comme toi au monde j'ai été
Et comme moi mort tu seras

Where you pass, I have passed
Where I have passed, you will pass
Like you, I have been in the world
And like me, dead you shall one day be

He knows our every step, and he went to death, as we will die, ahead of us. Let this not be Elizabeth's day. Let her follow you later, Lord, as one day we all will do.

Jesus Christ died on a cross and that kind of death ends in suffocation. The lungs cannot function any longer. You cannot draw a breath, and you die. It could not be said that Elizabeth in her state was untouched or unknown by the Lord to whom we lift prayers. That made the ordeal not one wit easier and not less an ordeal. But we knew we were praying to one about whom it was written: we have not a High Priest which cannot be touched with the feeling of our infirmities.

> For whatever reason God chose to make man as he is—limited and suffering and subject to sorrows and death—He had the honesty and the courage to take His own medicine. Whatever game He is playing with His creation, He has kept His own rules and played fair. He can exact nothing from man that He has not exacted from Himself. He has Himself gone through the whole of human experience, from the trivial irritations of family life and the cramping restrictions of hard work and lack of money to the worst horrors of pain and humiliation, defeat, despair, and death. When He was a man, He played the man.

The wise words of Dorothy Sayers.

We would have that much to place our trust in, and so it was.

8

A Gift of Life

MONDAY MAY 22 WAS my sixty-third birthday. I would go up as usual to see Elizabeth during visiting hours, which ran from 2 to 5 p.m. It would be an odd birthday, but things like that had receded in importance anyway.

It was a donor that we were praying for.

I had gone into our market town, Milly la Fôret, to pick up milk and other essentials. I had to get some money out of the cash machine and mail some letters, two errands overlapping in one direction in the village. It was a bright day, not cold and a touch spring like. My cell phone rang, and I answered it, noting a strange number. It was the surgeon's voice. "We have lungs. We are going in."

I nearly gasped for breath. "Will you start right away?" I asked. It was late morning.

"Yes. We are going to make this happen."

"I'll let you go, then. Thank you, thank you."

I felt like I had entered a different reality. I knew this was not victory, but I knew as well it was the path ahead that led away from death waiting in a hospital bed. I hadn't got the milk so to that mundane chore I turned my step. On the main market street who did I run into but the doughty neighbor so invested in praying Elizabeth back to health and supporting me. What were the odds of that! I told her the good news. She beamed. Alleluia. We hugged and I promised to stay in touch with any news.

I went into the shop to get milk and sundries. I made my way to the refrigerator case down a familiar aisle. I'm not sure I ever paid any attention to the fact that music was always being piped in as a dull background noise. But today I did. It was the familiar voice of Louis Armstrong. I kid you not. I joined with him and said to myself, "What a wonderful world." I cried with joy and took it as the message of angels sent to reassure me.

A trip to Marie Lannelongue was now off the plate. She would be in surgery for twelve hours. It was a time for prayer and communicating with family and friends. Uncharacteristically, my cell phone buzzed again. It was our good friend Eric Saunder, French photographer and colleague of Elizabeth in her work. Good Catholic companion. Could we have lunch? He happened to be in our neighborhood, en route to the Loire for a shoot at one of the chateaux where he was preparing a photographic book of their famous irises. Couldn't think of a reason to say no. It was just a waiting period now. It was my birthday, and I had just received the present of a lifetime.

We sat outside at a café under the trees. He was ecstatic to receive the good news. We ordered our food and sipped a glass of rosé in honor of Elizabeth as we waited. Who would walk up and sit down but Père Mercier and the wardens of the church, meeting over lunch on church business. I gave him the good news. What a well-organized happenstance, one might say, or the silently moving hand of God. My birthday present had arrived, the surgeons were at work, and we all pledged our prayers for their success and new life for Elizabeth.

I have yet not mentioned all the support we had been receiving from friends and family back home. Pledges of prayers and dedicated teams petitioning for Elizabeth. It would be good to let them know things were moving ahead. A donor had been found, and a double lung transplant was underway. This was an answer to prayer and a reason to continue as the doctors worked through the day and into the late evening. Family and friends were forbidden from visiting during this long ordeal, and there was nothing to be said at any rate. If the surgery was successful, she would be in a post-operative induced coma for several days at the least, all going well, and longer would be normal as well. This is a time for healing and recovery, and it cannot be rushed.

They had told us both prior to surgery that the drugs were very powerful that kept this state going, and that when in time it appeared she might awake it would be good if I were present. Patients do not know where they are, they will have been asleep for a long time, the aftereffects of the drugs are very strong, disorienting, even hallucinatory. This phase of the journey would have a life of its own.

The advice given to me by knowledgeable friends and by the nurses in the urgent arena she returned to, to her own bed again, was to speak and act as though she were awake and listening. It is hard to know how much of this gets through in its own special way and on its own special wavelength. I had selected key psalms to read. I found some favorite travel books and would just read long passages aloud. The nurses would smile or ignore me as into the air went long English-language narration from this or that book totally detached from affairs at hand. Wintering in Provence. The weekday market life in the Vaucluse. Napoleon's upbringing in Corsica. Recipes for a nice daube or a cassoulet from southwest France. Psalm 23, Psalm 80, Psalm 18.

It was also important to touch, caress, kiss, make human contact. A hand placed on a forehead can convey enormous reassurance. Each day she had a new hairdo, top knot here, side knot there, due to the tubes and various breathing apparatus needing to be negotiated. They would rearrange her legs and general posture to let the body pretend it was not stuck in one position, even as that nearly was so of course.

These were not peaceful days. No one knew whether the lungs would take hold, and whether she could begin to live again. The nurses refused to give information and refused to encourage beyond what the limitations of the situation would permit. Elizabeth was fighting for her life, in the silent fight that only her own body knew the precise details of.

Monday came and went as did Tuesday. The daily commuting is stressful, especially if you get into rush-hour traffic, which is not easy to predict or skirt. A forty-minute trip can turn into two hours. I was leaving Marcel daily and he needed his walks. The stress that had built up had not subsided during the coma period, because it had its own peculiar challenge. Would she make it in the end? How would I get the body back? Elizabeth had done her will and we had decided we would ask my brother Mark to do the funeral if it came to that. We had not discussed burial.

On Tuesday evening I realized I was beginning to panic and felt my strength failing. I called my brother Mark and asked that, if Elizabeth died, could he come and help me? He said, of course. Our housekeeper was a stalwart soul and with a heart as big as the sky. Her husband had survived a heart valve replacement that had put him in a similar post-surgery coma, and she would remind me of how strong he now was and how his life had been given back to him. Three and four times a day she would text me with encouraging messages and pledge her prayers and those of her kids and husband. I can recall phoning my mother and breaking down unexpectedly. As always, she was there for us. She had tracked the details of Elizabeth's condition with the dedication of a skilled researcher, from day one to today, and could be counted on always to know just what Elizabeth would happen to be explaining to her when they talked. That is a gift she still cherishes.

I awoke on Wednesday feeling like I had crossed a dark night of the soul, and I was able to re-summon strength. Some gifting I needed had arrived with the break of day and a fresh horizon before me. I drove up and got dressed and entered Elizabeth's room. The nurses seemed more inclined to offer support and encouragement. They could say that things were going as they should. That was reassuring and I believe they meant it truthfully to be so. I did our usual reading aloud and went back to take care of the dog.

The following day a thought occurred to me. When I was at Yale, I had a colleague and good friend whose wife had developed Alzheimer's disease. She was several years into that declining illness, and he was taking care of her at home still. Assisted living was not far off, though. He would feed and bathe her and always made an effort at cheerful communication even though she was responding very little, or in disconnected ways. It is a hard disease and requires tremendous patience. She was confined now to a special room in the house fitted out for her.

In the evenings before she went to bed, Lee would place his hand lovingly on her head. "We are going into King's College for Evensong. Can you hear the choir? Isn't the singing grand?" He would play some of that resplendent choral music and her eyes would light up and you could see her taking her seat in a warm chapel miles away across the ocean. She was alive to herself and to Lee and to the choir, if but for a moment. If he played country music from her small town in rural West Virginia, music she had not played since her childhood and might have thought she had never listened to in her life, her foot would skip, and one could see her raise herself up as if trying to dance. The needle of the Alzheimer record skips, but every now and then it finds a groove.

I asked the nurse if I could play music for Elizabeth. The idea frightened me a bit because I did not want to cause any harm and I was unsure what I would do if indeed she did show signs of recognition. She said, of course. Would she be there at the ready in case, after now four days of coma silence, Elizabeth responded? Yes, she nodded. I had several familiar tunes ready on my cell phone. The hymn *Prosternez-vous*, which I may respond to more than her, but which we know from French church. And the soundtrack music from *Cinema Paradiso* and *The Mission*, both by Ennio Morricone.

Certainly, one could sense that the music was doing something. Her eyes would try to move and react, and she lifted her chest a bit. It was all very strange and frightening in a way, like reanimation, which of course it was in fact. But it was the longer piece, and the one she loves the most, "Gabriel's Oboe" from *The Mission*, that brought forth her most sustained and obvious reaction. She sought to raise herself up. She stretched and strained. Her eyes flickered. I called the nurse to be sure this was all OK. I did not want to wake her up if it was not time and if this was preempting their protocols. No, all OK.

Then it occurred to me to ask her in my own voice, can you hear me? It's Chris. Squeeze my hand if you can hear me. She did. I felt instantly connected and felt strongly that now she would make it. The nurse just smiled, and we let her drop back into her coma state. Upon leaving that afternoon I decided I would take my special gauzy uniform home with me, as a memorial. They have plenty more at the ready and I wanted to remember this day.

9

Recovery

I STRONGLY FELT THAT Elizabeth had turned a corner. She was back in the land of the living, I believed, even as she was sleeping the deep sleep of recovering health and she was not yet alive to us as before.

I would search the Psalms for good lines befitting the situation Elizabeth had found herself in, and lines that would capture her plight. And that would speak both truthfully, hopefully. For the Psalms are calibrated for the deepest anguish, the most candidly spoken fear, the confessed sense of abandonment by God, unvarnished and unadorned. No wonder day by day and even hour by hour monks down the ages have asked them to replace whatever passions might arise naturally, because the Psalms through serial reading cover the waterfront and teach our passions and emotions how best to speak.

This is also why their sense of sequence seems sometimes mixed up to us. In pain, sequence is out of kilter. The book of Lamentations organizes its five strong laments according to the letters of the alphabet, and that in part because otherwise the here-and-there, up-and-down chaos of pain and fear and anger and loss would make no organized sense.

One of the Psalms that best captured this for me and which I read to Elizabeth daily was Psalm 116:

> I love the Lord, for he heard my voice;
> he heard my cry for mercy.
> Because he turned his ear to me,
> I will call on him as long as I live.

The cords of death entangled me,
  the anguish of the grave came over me;
  I was overcome by distress and sorrow.
Then I called on the name of the Lord:
  "Lord, save me!"

The Lord is gracious and righteous;
  our God is full of compassion.
The Lord protects the unwary;
  when I was brought low, he saved me.

Return to your rest, my soul,
  for the Lord has been good to you.

For you, Lord, have delivered me from death,
  my eyes from tears,
  my feet from stumbling,
that I may walk before the Lord
  in the land of the living.

I doubt one can improve on this in terms of economy, straight-talking, and truth. I believe it says it all. One gets out of its way and lets it have voice. A voice from the ages of ages.

Friday and Saturday would be quiet days as the nurses did their monitoring, and the coma did its silent healing. Psalms could be read and a body spoken to and touched. But Elizabeth would awake to life again. We just could not know when.

I was conscious of wanting to be present for the reasons already mentioned: the sense of anxiety and disorientation when at last she came back into consciousness for good. I would call and try to underscore this, but it seemed less decisive than I had been led to believe.

Sunday came. Our church was there to greet me and receive the news that new lungs had arrived and that my wife had squeezed my hand in recognition and that we now believed she would live and rejoin us. The week past had been an eternity. There was a sense of relief and gratitude that God would let us see her with us again. We longed to have things back to where there were, and now even higher and healthier, given the news of new lungs and steady recovery.

Elizabeth had helped plan an extended holiday in Provence for a very close friend from Vanderbilt days, which she and her now grown daughter could celebrate, mom and daughter together. We were having beautiful May weather and of course even more so down south where they were. Carol had been staying in touch during this important week and had done so continually previously. The news of a successful transplant and slow but sure recovery was received with joy. Carol, an experienced cancer nurse herself, and her daughter Austin, were to be in Paris on the Sunday before flying back. Could we organize a rendezvous at Marie Lannelongue that afternoon?

They arrived by Uber. I was awaiting them when the car pulled up. You must declare yourself a relative, so Elizabeth's new "sister" Carol donned the surgical room garments familiar to her, and the three of us made our way to Elizabeth's room. Only two persons are allowed to visit at a time, and I wanted Austin and Carol to go first. Austin, when an infant, had a close rub with death and Elizabeth had been present with her friend Carol in the urgent care unit at the time. What a propitious turn of events that would find the infant, now a beautiful young adult woman, accompanying her mother to support Elizabeth in her version of the same.

The nurse came back to take me to a waiting room I did not know existed. It had been me alone visiting during this time, or Elizabeth's Paris friends on their own. As I was taking my seat, she mentioned in passing that Elizabeth had woken and was talking and getting reoriented to being alive. What!? Please go get Austin and let us change places. Happy to oblige, Austin went off to jog on a nearby trail we had located when she arrived, to return later. She had been able to say hello and headed off to lace up her jogging shoes.

I was so excited to hear that Elizabeth had woken up, but I had recalled the comment that it would be best if I or a loved one was there. I had frequently called the nurses station precisely to see if they could better anticipate this timing so I could be present. Obviously, it is a hard thing to predict, so I understood. I followed the nurse and arrived at the threshold to Elizabeth's room and looked in.

There she was, sitting up in bed. Carol was beaming. Elizabeth looked dazed and happy, a bit frightened, unsteady but alive. I entered the room, kissed her, and took my familiar place at the side of her bed.

She could talk well enough but was stunned and scared. She wasn't sure where she was. She explained bits of it to us as we enjoyed just seeing her alive, all of us together.

When she woke up, she had no idea where she was and why she was there, or even that she'd had surgery. She thought perhaps she was in a mental hospital, where for some reason she had been committed. Her arms had been constrained so her tubes would not be pulled out by mistake, or in confusion if she awoke, so perhaps that gave her the sense of a committal. The drugs are very powerful and at times the nurses appeared to her as monsters.

They asked her to reach to her chest and feel the bandages. You have had surgery and a lung transplant. She had been asleep for six days. Slowly it would sink in.

Carol the nurse was impressed with the technology and general operation of the unit, surveying the landscape with practiced eye. I would explain my silent routines over the past days, all our friends' concerns, how Marcel was doing, how things were at the house. It was hard for her to pretend she could carry on a regular conversation, and she was happy to listen, look over her room, and puzzle out her survival. Elizabeth is a private person, and this was as exposed a context and experience as one could possibly imagine. Twelve hours of being carved open and new lungs sewed in, her chest stitched back together, lying in a bed with a maze of tubes, and machines chirping and humming on every corner. From time to time she would burst out, unexpectedly, *embrasse-moi*. It was a place in time we will never forget. Our girl was back again. Carol said goodbye and I kissed Elizabeth and promised to return tomorrow. Marcel and I danced his version of a jig when I got home. He would hear her voice and smell her smell again. I think he knew she was back in the land of the living.

If you know anything about the French, it is that their school system and general upbringing asks children to grow up, expects them to be strong and attentive to authority, assumes children can sit quietly and keep themselves occupied, and those children who are exceptions to this are thought of as unfortunate or hampered or poorly raised. Adults do not helicopter. They have their own lives and expect the school system to do its part. Their own job as parents is to quietly discourage self-indulgence and excuse-making, and to proudly hope that their children will find a way to be at peace with themselves and in their own skin.

So, it would be but a few days before it would be time for Elizabeth to get up and move to a new zone in the hospital. She had new lungs, and she needed to put them to work. Long years of going downhill needed to be offset right away with fresh patterns, exercise, good food, rest of course. The horizons once dark and setting were alive now with light and dawning.

The nurses here were great. A different breed for a different task. She had a bright room and could look at the green spaces from her window. It was a pleasure to visit. The nurses like to work on their English, if inclined. One sturdy and strong young Black nurse, her hair in long dreadlocks, had an athletic posture and athletic movements. One day she asked in French about US professional football. Her favorite team, she said, was the Seattle Seahawks. We learned she played in a women's US-style football league, helmets and pads and hard tackling. She proudly told us she was a linebacker. Good for a nurse in the rehab unit.

They had her up and walking the hallways within several days. Soon she could walk outside in the parkland that so nicely surrounded the hospital. What a great idea to have that there. One day the nurses surprised her. A singer was at her door. Songs from Gershwin and American musicals were her specialty. Can you imagine that? A private concert, modest but professional, just for Elizabeth. A woman lay chaplain would visit from the *aumonerie* (hospital chaplaincy). Our clergy at home had contacted the chaplaincy unit at the hospital. Yes, the French can separate church and state, but sickness and dying also shake their head at that and the French defer with heads lowered in respect.

My parents had promised to visit us at some point in time, when we left for France in late 2015. We knew of course that this would be hard to do. My dad's physical health was slowing down, and it was getting harder for him to walk, even as he attacked the daily route with vigor and determination. I missed him and his constant optimism. On the wall of his office was a small plaque. I made note of it after his funeral as we roamed about the house and thought of him and his ways. It says a lot about the man he was and where his trust lay.

> Good morning, this is God.
> I will be handling all your problems today.
> I will not need your help, so have a good time.
> I love you.

It takes an unusual kind of strength to surrender to a greater power than one's own. It gave him in turn the strength to be strong and confident and to think of others first.

After Dad died, my brother Pete took over and wanted to bring Mom to France. The trip was planned with the knowledge of Elizabeth's condition, but without predicting the surgery that had taken place. The timing was about perfect. They arrived as Elizabeth was wrapping up the rehab, which took place for only about ten days. She made great progress. We went straight to see her after their flight had deposited them at Orly, halfway between Courances and Marie Lannelongue.

My mom is extraordinary. Loyal, smart, a fighter, let's get the job done. She had studied the details of Elizabeth's condition like a hawk. Had watched films on the smallest of research advances. Learned all about the NIH and its brilliant Christian head, Francis Collins. Tracked our progress and decline with an attentive heart and ear. It was fitting that she could be there and could watch us bring Elizabeth home.

One thing I wanted to see was the helicopter pad. I had got to know this four-story transplant hospital well. I had walked its nice gardens, eaten in its snack shop and bought papers for Elizabeth there. I knew many of the nurses and doctors by sight or more directly. Walking the corridors with Elizabeth during her rehab I realized the route from roof to restricted floor two must be easy to examine. It was. So hard to believe that from a hospital bed, just barely surviving, a team had placed her in a slatted life flight conveyance, inflated the sealed chambers around her, immobilizing her so the machines could continue to keep her alive, and with blades whirring lifted off from one suburban hospital into the Paris skies and deposited her right here. A team of trained men I would likely never meet, who did this job 24/7, who, alongside doctors, nurses, surgeons, rehab teams, had saved my wife's life.

A French miracle.

10

Mont St-Victoire

I HAVE WRITTEN THIS chronicle during a winter stay in South Carolina. Elizabeth and I spent Christmas through March 2019 at a condominium we own in Sea Pines, Hilton Head. We used the time to look at houses we might buy, as we considered moving back to the US at the end of the year.

I used the time to process the events we had shared together, and to write down what you have read. I have familiar writing routines from my work as an author. I would write each morning and come down and share my work with Elizabeth. I would cry and relive difficult moments now behind us both.

I was also reading aloud to give Elizabeth a flavor of my thoughts, as the plan was for her to come alongside my brief chapters with reflections of her own. I really wanted to hear "her side of the story" and it also belonged to what I thought was a good design for this book.

2019 was the year of our gradual adjustment to the idea of leaving our French home and returning to the United States. My mother died in 2019 after a slow decline and hospice care. It was a mercy. She missed her husband of seventy years of marriage.

Elizabeth had thrown herself back in her work at French Affaires. It was her strong instinct after the successful return to life in May 2017. We planned a great Normandy trip that summer, and she enjoyed her return to health. I went to an international meeting in Berlin, where we had been in the early days of our marriage. We did our favorite visit to Provence. Her new lungs were bringing back energy. The doctors had insisted the long slog of six years of LAM was over and it was time to breathe and use her new French lungs to the full.

In 2018 we had a great holiday in Burgundy, and then a week in the Gard. We visited my relatives in the Rhine Valley, stopping in Alsace along the way. Elizabeth had a stunning culinary event in our backyard and in the chateau of Courances grounds. A Normandy French Affaires trip was in the fall. Marcel was competing in field trials in his native Auvergne region, where we found a lovely auberge. He was runner-up for best under-threes at a competition held in Cognac. I got my French hunting license in the Seine-et-Marne Department. I taught as a visiting professor in Paris at Centre Sevres, the Jesuit seminary, pushing my language competence to the limit. We visited Corsica to reconnoiter and plan for a future French Affaires offering.

2019 was equally busy, with trips to Brittany to visit friends, and a lovely stay in southwest France to see Eric and Claire Sander and for me to do some language work.

As usual, that summer we visited Provence and took in our favorite spots. It was so great to have my dear wife operating with new lungs and able to do things she'd had to stop doing for so many years.

One previous summer in 2016 we had stayed in Chateauneuf la Rouge, just east of Aix-en-Provence. I am an avid climber. I took two groups up the Grossglockner in my twenties (the highest peak in Austria, at 3,800 meters). I went to the top of the Zugspitze with my Weimaraner dog in my late thirties. I climbed Ben Nevis in Scotland in my fifties. I wanted to go up Mont Sainte-Victoire that summer. It is about a thousand meters, but from a sea-level start. Elizabeth stayed with Marcel at the foot on the trail, on the south side of the crest. I recall it as a kindness on her part, as she had climbed the famously painted Cézanne site in her marathon-runner days, and as a frequent visitor to the area, going back to her time in college.

So, we had it in view to climb together that summer of 2019. We left from the car park on the northern ascent, from the Barrage de Bimont. The ascent was shorter but as such, also steeper. I can see my lovely girl making her way with her customary steady pace. I am more restless and would push ahead, pause and wait for her. She faltered and wondered about the final ascent to the summit. I could see her struggling. I remembered the sage advice of the Austrian guides. "We go slow." As slow as is possible so that there is no stopping, and the lungs can find their rhythm. I adjusted my pace to match hers.

There is a priory at the top. To reach the massive steel cross and weather station at the very summit there are cables to help with handholds.

The path just about goes away. That was too much. Having stared death in the face, the world becomes more fragile and danger more real. We said our prayers together in the chapel and returned to the steady earth below. Elizabeth had her victory. We had a shared victory. Her wish to make her new self stand on the top of that favorite mountain came true. She looked down on a new world below.

The Breath of French Air had carried her to the top.

11

Victory's Next Laps

I HAD WAITED TO write the previous section, what I envisioned would be the final chapter of a chronicle called "A Breath of French Air." What could be more fitting than a final climb up a mountain called Victory, a return for Elizabeth to health, and to a place she held dear over the many years of her life in France.

In my mind's eye, I also thought that the victory climb would become the incentive for Elizabeth to put pen to paper, and to record how she had marched through fiery trials to a helicopter ride with a garden-hose-sized tube oxygenating her blood, to a surgical theater, to six days in reanimation, to new life. The climb up Mont Sainte-Victoire matching her own grueling physical challenge over six years, and a final victory at last.

However, she never wrote her side of the story. I suppose there are several possible reasons for that. And they may overlap.

She told a friend she worried that French lungs ought to go to French citizens. Who was she publicly to chronicle a victory that might rightly belong to someone else, who perhaps had got moved down the queue so she could live?

I have also noted how much she immediately threw herself into her work. She wanted to make up for lost time. She wanted French Affaires to bubble with the new life that had been granted her. And so that is where she placed her energy after the May 2017 transplant.

I also wonder whether a victory like hers sent her into a place she had to go alone, no matter how much I sought to be with her and did indeed go with her, did indeed suffer her suffering. I have "my side of the story" that was our story as a couple, and that overlapped in ways that marriage mysteriously compels, the one for the other. Yet there is a place where, before God and before the reality of our death, we must go alone. She had entered that place, in a hospital bed, feet from the surgical theater, with nothing between her and her death except another death, one that would bring her lungs by urgent vehicle transport, from some scene of dying somewhere else in France.

Such an experience deserves to be called singular, a solitude of God and you.

My father and mother were married for seven decades. They did everything together. Were far more intertwined than most couples, for better or for worse, and were less independent in ways that were perforce so for Elizabeth and me, who married after decades of work and self-direction.

Yet when my father died, when the sepsis in his gut became so unbearable, he wanted to spare my mother. He wanted to be alone and go home to his Lord. The time comes where death is unshareable. It is for the loved one—someone who has been your whole life—to now cross over a bar alone, because death is as singular as birth. In my father's case, a priest for one day longer than he was a husband, he was prepared to cross that bar.

And, so, Elizabeth had to be ready as well. And she was. I can now wonder how I might have thought anyone could tell that story, so singular and real was the proximity of a death quite likely to be her own. Mont Sainte-Victoire was an important milepost, but it paled in comparison to going under a knife to receive a set of lungs someone had died to give her. If indeed the surgery succeeded.

When she awoke after six days, her first thought, filled with the powerful drugs, was that I had committed her. That she was in a mental hospital. And in some very real way the experience was insane. Insanely blessed and graced by God.

So, for whatever reason, the story remains my own to tell. A story of a singular journey to death's door, and a miracle of new life, for the love of my life.

I am writing this now five years after the Breath of French air filled her new lungs. She died on September 23, 2021, almost to the day ten years after receiving the original LAM diagnosis. Her new lungs were no match for a disease no one had heard of even two years previously: COVID-19. Delta variant. Killer of my precious wife. Jeanne Elizabeth New Seitz, age fifty-six.

Jeanne Elizabeth New Seitz
18 December 1964 - 23 September 2021
Ma Femme
Belle Forte Fidele
Le Roi d'Amour est Mon Berger

12

Death Arrives

It is a great and true joy to write an account of victory through hardship. One can relive the horrible moments, times of fear and doubt, knowing the outcome has been secured at last. The momentum is obvious enough and it carries the story forward. One can recall forgotten episodes and linger over frightening details, knowing the final victory is propelling the story along to its victorious conclusion.

My wife died four years ago. Her transplant was seven years ago. One can gloss over the fine print of medicines made necessary by the intrusion of a new set of lungs, regimens to be scrupulously observed, the regular follow-up visits and difficult times that mark the days of the transplant survivor. The sure, grasped victory gives one a wider vision of gratitude, and a relief that death did not come. Months of decline and decay vanish before the miracle of a life handed back and a new start given.

So, what does it mean to bask in that joy, to experience a fresh start, to be brought forth from the jaws of death, only to have a trap door open and a life cruelly snuffed out? COVID did its work very quickly. Six years of decline with LAM disease collapsed into a series of weeks. The same tubes, same ICUs, same worried nurses, same stop-and-start hopelessness and hope. The same brave woman I love and who was given back to me, once more thrown into the breach.

Because of the ravages of COVID internationally, my wife's passion for French Affaires and its routines had to be put on hold. Trips planned and queued up at the ready were forced to be deferred, 2019 giving way to 2020, and on to 2021. This may sound somewhat insignificant, given the stakes, but no one knew the virulence of this newcomer disease and how long it would hang on. What wreckage it would leave in its wake.

And French Affaires wasn't and isn't a business. It was Elizabeth's passion, love, gift to others, which brought a gift back to her.

I cannot rehearse the horrors of her last days and the sheer agony she endured. The very fact of having to go back yet again into this hellish terrain is itself a cause for silence. We both knew it in some terrible recess of our consciousness. Oh, no. Here comes death. After all that has been endured. After years of decline. After the victory I at least wanted to proclaim with all my soul, from the mountaintop of our climb in Provence, and on these pages.

I will say just one thing. Part of the victory is knowing you have shared something, have been somewhere strange and terrible together, have communicated man to woman, and woman to man, with everything you have and with all the strength you can muster, into the very jaws of death itself. That marks you. Changes you. Defines you thereafter in ways you cannot describe because it is a communion of flesh and blood itself, stronger than words or our best efforts at telling and recalling and retelling. You lie next to the flesh and blood survivor, in the night, and know something has been achieved that will never go away, because it was such an ordeal to be shared and to have endured together. You have lived through the "for worse," the "poorer," the "in sickness," and even "the death"—a death that stalked and was yet halted. Having reached the end of the line, and having then been brought into open water, by a miracle, made us a different man and woman, forever. My wife Elizabeth and her husband Chris re-formed.

When the true and final "death do us part" arrived, after that shared experience of near death, what was truly horrible is that we could not share, could not go into the breach side-by-side, not this time.

I had been in France running a trip for Elizabeth to calm her shattered nerves. The doctors thought this was best, and the plan was for her to go into out-patient dialysis. But in a few days, it was clear things were not going to end that way. I called Carol, the woman who had been with Elizabeth when she came out of the Paris reanimation, and she arrived with her godly ICU skills. She bathed Elizabeth and readied her to meet her earthly bridegroom and her heavenly Lord.

I had not been privy to the discussions Elizabeth had had about end of life. I arrived from Burgundy exhausted but still hopeful. She had been a warrior, and she had won. When I entered the room and saw her with her C-pap mask, forcing air into her lungs, I steadied my nerves and said all would be well. Again. As in Paris.

I was wrong, though it was only clear on retrospection. The intubation she agreed to, that she knew would mean her dying was now a fact, I took to mean the end of a horrible suffering that would hopefully buy her time. She reached up to place her hand on my cheek, and I thought, she is putting on her war paint again, she will again be victorious, we will again have a new and fresh season we had both longed to have, at last.

But she was saying goodbye, forever.

I arrived the next day and the doctors told me what Elizabeth knew and what they knew, but it hit me like a ton of bricks. They would turn off the life support and she would slowly breath her last. The Breath of French Air would cease.

I went into a place reserved for husband and wife. For a priest. How selfish it would be, some part of me said, to burden her with my grief, to the degree she was conscious of me in her intubated state. An awkward chaplain arrived, and I could see that. I asked for oil, anointed her and gave her last rites. I prayed in the French language we shared. Again and again all I could say was "I love you" "I'll always love you," "You are my girl forever." I wanted her to go without any burden.

Those who know what it is like to have machines giving life be turned off know that it can go several different ways. My sweet girl. The lines that furrowed her brow in life went quiet. Her breathing was at times quiet and at times gurgling. I thought, "I want her breath in my lungs," and wondered why the air I was drawing into myself was so fragrant and beautiful. And then almost imperceptibly she breathed her last.

Ma femme. Belle. Forte. Fidèle.

13

Encore Mont St-Victoire

So, THERE IS NO happy ending for this story as it had originally been conceived. No happy denouement. No victory as previously proclaimed on mountaintop. No decline reversed. No lungs arriving by urgent vehicle in France to change the dire landscape into a place of blossoms. My warrior wife had fought her last battle in this life.

I'd like to say something that makes sense but most of the chronicling is now in a language I am trying to learn. That comes to me as so much wailing incomprehensibility and dull pain. Fear of sleep because I do not want to wake up and face a truth sleep had hidden for a while.

I have taken over French Affaires, Elizabeth's passion and in many ways her second self. I know many of the paths, the vendors, the museums, the guides, the familiar cafes and restaurants that brought us joy. Our life in France was our life. It was a life snatched from death. That miracle stands.

To move forward, however, I needed help from friends in France. Heaven has provided them. The garden specialist, culinary and wine specialist, Paris *incontournable* specialist. I did not want her passion to die alongside her, and I wanted to stabilize the ship as best I could. Much of this had to be done as a matter of urgency, with trips already on the books. Elizabeth talked to my brother when I was in Burgundy, and he was convinced she was handing French Affaires into my care. When I sat on her ICU bed and said I did not want to go, she said in her customary way, "You have to."

I have found a guide, Maud Hacker, who knew Elizabeth. Not well, but they shopped together ("she bought that top I wanted") and I found

Elizabeth's emails in which they had been planning a perfume workshop for her clients.

Perhaps a story helps toward a clarity I am seeking.

I needed to go to Provence for a language immersion trip Elizabeth had clients for in May. I asked Maud to come and help me. She brought her ten-year-old daughter, and her mother joined us to help with child-care, and for a holiday for herself.

Of course, I know the area well and began looking for houses to rent. I shared my findings with the threesome. They especially liked a house, sunny and bright, just north of Aix. Its signature feature was the looming Mont Sainte-Victoire, facing down on us from the south.

Maybe we could also go for a climb, mother and daughter asked? Just a break when the trip research was taken care of.

I flew to Paris. After my arrival and a day to recover from jet lag, we loaded our bags and headed by fast train to Aix.

After several days of visits and research for the coming language immersion trip, we got our free day. Off we went to climb the summit of memories and victory, my life with Elizabeth stretching behind and before us. A climb that had shown God's great gift of new lungs and new life.

We found the car park at Barrage de Bimont. The path was familiar but also a bit different. Did we cross the dam last time? My memory was a bit faulty. We found the blue flashes marking the trail and slowly made our way. Ten-year-old advancing in leaps and bounds, me staying close to make sure no slips and falls, mother bringing up the rear.

Yes, my girl was beside me. My Elizabeth New Seitz. "Sing to the Lord a *New* Song" I can hear my own mom say with a smile at our reception dinner, happy to see us married, happy to recite Psalm 96 in tribute.

As we climbed and progressed, I realized what an arduous journey it was in fact. Mom was winded. February was windy and colder as we climbed, but I was in a sweat. We neared the final assault after ninety minutes' climb. I sensed that it was getting to be a bit much for mom. Daughter was ever-ready to move on.

There is a place where the path levels out, where you can see the steep final assault ahead. The cross high above, the profile of the old priory. The weather station with its vigilant team on watch.

I took my ten-year-old companion aside, distanced from mom by fifty meters behind us, and said I wanted to speak to her for a brief moment. The bustling and energetic face, intelligent and beautiful, looked up at me.

"You have your life ahead of you" I said in French. "You will be back here. The summit will always be there. You will conquer it one day soon. Do your mom a kindness, and say you are happy and ready to turn around and descend. She is tired."

That happy face looked at me and nodded. Yes.

And so, the final summit of Elizabeth and my journeying is left to the two of us, to the sweet and tired breath of our conversations as we climbed that day. To the victory given by the One who gave her life and breath and who made my life forever hers and ours.

Part Three

The Love That Grief Is

The Love That Grief Is

The Hearth in the Soul

ELIZABETH AND I HAD a friend from the Dordogne who was an acclaimed documentary writer and producer. After Elizabeth's sudden death, I decided to share with her the account I had prepared, "A Breath of French Air," and to get her advice. It is obviously a very personal, painful story and I am close to the details, as close as is possible.

Victor Hugo wrote of the death of his wife, "You are no longer where you were, but you are everywhere where I am."

I wanted her perspective. It was shortly after Elizabeth died.

She said that I would, of course, need to fashion a conclusion. One that would consider that the Victory climb had become a descent into death from COVID, a disease no one had known before or anticipated its ravages. The cruel reversal of fortune—miraculous life-saving surgery, followed by a new disease's assault—would ask for a story hard to complete. Indeed, what would one say?

The walk up to the summit of Mont St-Victoire with my friend and her daughter spoke to me with its own voice. I have sought to hear it. To allow it to speak to me and to guide me as I seek to do what our Dordogne friend suggested.

What I have learned is that it is impossible to write a conclusion adapted to a story of victory, especially a victory as described for Elizabeth and for me. The sheer bliss of having someone brought back to life and given over to you for years to come.

That is because grief is nothing but a love that never ends and that enriches and deepens over time. I want to speak about that reality. It has come to me slowly, through searing pain, agonizing confusion, and disbelief, loss of any spatial recognition, and a void that has spoken to me louder than anything I have ever experienced in my life.

Two final stanzas from a poem a close friend hand-wrote to me in the months after losing Elizabeth, from the poet John O'Donohue. He writes this:

> It becomes hard to trust yourself
> All you can depend on now is that
> Sorrow will remain faithful to itself
> More than you, it knows its way
> And will find the right time
> To pull and pull the rope of grief
> Until that coil of tears
> Has reduced to its last drop.
>
> Gradually, you will learn acquaintance
> With the invisible form of your departed;
> And when the work of grief is done
> The wound of loss will heal
> And you will have learned
> To wean your eyes
> From that gap in the air
> And be able to enter the hearth
> In your soul where your loved one
> Has awaited your return
> All the time.

So, in this third section I want to explore the reality of this—the love that grief is and that grief uncovers—as best I can. In so doing, I hope to say things that may be of help to those who know what I have been through, though of course with their own unique experience. We have fingerprints that are unique. The fingerprint of love is unique, and because of that, so, too, the loss of a loved one.

> To wean your eyes
> From that gap in the air
> And be able to enter the hearth
> In your soul where your loved one
> Has awaited your return
> All the time.

One thing I must emphasize. When my wife died, well-meaning people sent me sensitive, personal accounts of losing a loved one in death. Who cannot learn something from C. S. Lewis and his experience?

Or another precious and sturdy chronicle of loss from this or that dear friend?

Speaking for myself, these only underscored the particularity of my loss, and the difference between how others faced the void of a harsh departure of someone dearly loved, and cared for—unto death—and my own version of that.

I say this at the outset to confess my aim is only to speak about a loss unique and particular to me. In "A Life Lived Well in France" I wanted to take LAM out of play so as to dwell on a very rich experience with my struggling, strong, and valiant wife, as we had "the time of our life," despite the hardship.

The "time of our life" *after her death* has a mirror image, by the grace of God, with *the time with LAM* recorded in chapters above. That truth has come to me slowly.

It involves, in both cases, the cultivation of memory. In what follows I will describe why, in the particularities of my life, that has been hard. Others will have their particular and unique sense of challenge.

Elizabeth, with me following her strength and grace, and summoning my own, transcended the travails of a disease without a cure through the ministrations of life shared in France. I know no better way to say that.

Her love of France and the love it returned to her, defeated LAM disease in its final, most virulent form. She became who God wanted her to be, and he knew she would be found safe and contented in his eternal care. Her life was saved by France, French lungs and an experience in the final years of LAM greater than the sum of all that preceded. In her life and, with me alongside her and praying for victory, in my own life.

What I want to speak about now is the transcendence of this strength and life, after her death, greater than COVID in the same way that it was greater than LAM. The "life lived well in France" occupies the territory of the first, and the chronicle I write now, about "the hearth of the soul," speaks of the second.

God seeks us in both terrains, and, because he has inhabited all disease, death, pain, excruciating loss, he will bring them all under a single victorious cross, empty tomb, and resurrected new life, where he has awaited our return all the time.

1

An Unhappy Business

A SUDDEN, TRAUMATIC DEATH means that nothing is in place. "Unhappy business" is my shorthand for this: all the things that must be taken care of, at the very moment when the pain and confusion of loss are at their greatest.

Elizabeth had faced the near-death experience of transplantation after the ravages of LAM. Sitting in her bed, coached by a friend and legal aid over the phone, she hand-wrote a will. That would be the extent of readying to die at that time—under pressing circumstances—should she not live.

And because she survived this ordeal, and lived another four years, we were not inclined to anticipate the kind of sudden death that would be her fate. She was a fifty-six-year-old survivor of LAM disease with new lungs and a new life snatched from the jaws of death. She was highly organized and no stranger to hard work but planning for a death was simply not the world we were living in after her return to life.

A further particularity that marked our situation was that we had become, happily, the best companions on a very hard journey. We had entered a special terrain and one that could only be shared, husband and wife. She told very few people she had LAM disease and did not want to give public evidence of it. The only first-row observers of what we went through were French friends. Our neighbors, church members, pharmacy assistants, area nurses. And this only in the months running up to the transplant, where her respiratory assistance was obvious for all to see.

Very few people knew she was having a lung transplant. Our life had re-centered itself inside France and their healthcare system. And she was private and independent. Our language was French in these circumstances.

The character of our life was such that, when we did decide to return to the United States, we had formed a relationship that was private, husband and wife. We had found a new language. We intended our home and our return to maintain the life we had in France, but with a US home base.

COVID arrived just three months after our return. The transatlantic shipment of our goods was slowed by the disease, and we found ourselves sequestered from a community we had not got to know, and that we did not intend to eclipse the life we planned to continue in France. I was approaching retirement age and would simply be bringing my final PhD students across the finish line. I imagined us continuing our French life.

I have spoken of the messiness of Elizabeth's final days, and of my swift return to the US to be with her in what turned out to be a silent and terrible ordeal of dying.

You are asked to begin making decisions. In our case, about things we had not discussed. Where she would be buried. Will. Body. Casket. Funeral service. Obituary. The transfer of her business to me. Months of dealing with her goods, and her estate.

Those reading this summary will have their own particular experience to relate to. The amount of work required is overwhelming. Given our private life, and our lack of any genuine community, the bulk of this fell to me. Our third floor was full, top-to-bottom, with affairs that had been gathered from storage in Dallas belonging to Elizabeth, our house in France, goods that were part of our shared life in Preston Hollow that did not get shipped across the ocean.

I spent four months handling things that I had never seen before. Her vast book collection. Memories and mementos that represented the growing up of a young girl, through college, through graduate school, through a decade of work in corporate life, and then finally joining up with our married life thirteen years earlier. Clothing, shoes, toiletries, perfumes, handbags, gloves, hats, paintings, precious jewelry, outerwear, scarves—much of it being handled by me for the first time. My wife loved clothing, books, memorabilia and she threw nothing away. I was handling her, in her absence, and I only shared this work when exhausted or confused.

The amount of stemware, China, flatwear, silver, and crystal was staggering. Much of this belonged to her work with French Affaires and the entertaining it entailed. And all of it had to be sorted through.

Elizabeth's privacy extended to her family, and I sought to honor that.

Again, this will be familiar territory for those who are grieving a lost loved one and also facing mountains of "unhappy business." This work has to be done.

My unhappy business took the form of having a wife who survived years of hard work dealing with LAM, a victory in France among our friends there, a return to COVID and death, in a place that was not our home. We had a large southern-style plantation home on the Okatie River (Lowcountry South Carolina), which was never meant to be the home of a grieving widower and the dog she left behind. It was like a haunted house, because we had only hidden from COVID there and carried on as best we could, under circumstances that were bringing the entire world to heel.

Elizabeth knew COVID was a killer, given her kidneys and the drugs fighting rejection, now part of her daily regimen. Killed her, it did.

I could say more, but what I am expressing belongs to a larger theme. There are necessary chores to attend to when a loved one dies. That job was hard and lonely, in my case, carried out in a strange land of our only-becoming-acquainted return. Helpers there were, but that big house was my job. It was not a place I could stay after losing her. Yet the work to clear it out, finalize the work necessary to put it on the market, and settle Elizabeth's vast estate moved along with its own inexorable tidal flow. This flow becomes a stream of dying water, with currents carrying one along and eddies to get trapped and weary in. One pushes ahead. The alternative is collapse and something like death.

I am sure many people handle this "unhappy business" differently than I did. But the larger theme is this: At some point one is about the business of closure. As the body goes in a box and is placed in the ground, so, too, myriad other jobs must be put to rest.

Inside of that is the wailing on the carpet, and the sense of pain and void so vast it cannot be fathomed but only endured. It is a drum beat below all the unhappy business, which that unhappy but necessary work cannot drown out. Hauling down trash bags of goods from the third floor, day after day, brings physical, moral, and emotional arthritis. You are lost in some foreign land.

And because the tidal force of having all this work to do becomes all consuming, drowning one, lost in its breakers, the cruciality of bringing order to bear consumes the mind and body and spirit.

And all this is going in the wrong direction when it comes to grief itself.

Grief is a form of love. It is the love that persists and grows as the loved one becomes real and true in a different but more permanent and precious expression of who they now are, for you, forever.

There is a potential misstep here. Because it comes alongside the closure work—this unhappy business that must be wrapped up and moved beyond—one might imagine that the loved one is going to be swept up into this tide as well. In other words, it is very easy to start thinking that just as this closure work must be finished and put into the past, so too must my loved one, and my love.

The language people sometimes use can suggest precisely this misstep: "It's time to move on." This might well make sense for some kinds of grief with which I am unaware, but it is language that, if internalized, is defeating and deeply injurious. Elizabeth isn't a set of chores to get finished, even as chores needed to be finished up as part of the unhappy business of death. There is a trauma needing healing.

People say "time heals all wounds" and "you'll get over her" and they mean well. In reality, it isn't so much you they are trying to help but some part of themselves. They feel uneasy about the fact of death and the extent of pain that losing someone entails—the particular story of your particular life.

Trauma does not conform to timetables or punch-lists.

"Sorrow will remain faithful to itself / More than you, it knows its way."

2

The Problem of "Spatial Recognition"

John O'Donohue writes this as the opening stanza of the poem cited above.

> When you lose someone you love.
> Your life becomes strange,
> The ground beneath you becomes fragile,
> Your thoughts make your eyes unsure;
> And some dead echo drags your voice down
> Where words have no confidence.

One of the struggles I have had to face is spatial. I live in a space in the United States that does not carry memories of my life with Elizabeth. Or minimal ones. The ironic fact that we collected so many of our memories in a foreign country, where further, her life was saved, has meant it has been difficult for me to process grief. Grief is occasioned by memories, and memories are occasioned in the most immediate sense, spatially.

The "life lived well in France" was meant to continue alongside our life in the US, and to be the shared life of both memory and ongoing enjoyment for us both—more rich, given her survival after a six-year decline. France was the place of survival, new life, and rich experiences.

The form this life was to take revolved around the continuation of French Affaires travel, the successful business Elizabeth founded, and that thrived when we lived in France. French Affaires is more than excellent trips, it is also friends and fellowship, nurtured over the years.

Elizabeth had organized trips all over France, including the Island of Corsica. The ones she was preparing after our return here included Normandy, Burgundy/Lyon, southwest France, Burgundy/Lyon II, and

Paris at the Holidays—a perennial favorite. In addition, the Garden Club of Dallas had requested a private trip.

Due to the outbreak of COVID, these trips had to be postponed. This made life especially hard for Elizabeth. French Affaires was a business that brought her joy, allowed her to speak French, and which was now connected to our rich life as we had experienced it together. So, it was a disappointment to me as well. I had planned my retirement around our returning to France, including years beyond French Affaires (which was also a good deal of work).

One consequence of this is that Elizabeth was thrown into a limbo. No one knew anything about COVID, and what we now know is that this state of affairs would persist, even when vaccines and various treatments had come into play, with "experts" claiming they were on top of things. Trips, too, went into limbo. Clients wanted what Elizabeth offered, and everyone had to put their life on hold and wait.

2020 passed. 2021 was still under the COVID shadow. We went on a personal visit to the south of France, and our former home in Courances, south of Paris, in July of 2021. Fortunately, Elizabeth made a podcast in a lavender field below Les Baux-de-Provence, with an artisan who was preserving the art of weaving lavender wands. I can still watch it and marvel at her poise, and the simple fact of hearing her voice and seeing her be her. I will say more about this below.

She would die in a hospital bed in the ICU at Charleston Medical Hospital only two months later.

It would be our last time together in France.

Because of the anxiety of having these trips—her life—on hold, the doctors would be concerned that this was hindering the recovery underway, after contracting COVID. Her body had lungs that gave her "the breath of French air," and that were being encouraged to become her own lungs through strong medicines. Her case was not a typical one—whatever that might mean in the face of this diabolical killing-machine virus.

She asked me to go and take one trip, and the doctors thought it would be a good respite for her mind. I have spoken about this above. My point here is only to underscore how much France had become a part of our life. And how, in turn, it would make the space of my present living a difficult place to "find" Elizabeth. To grieve her loss, means being in space where I recognize her, see her, recall her.

When I returned and she died—with all the shock and trauma that followed—I had to make decisions about French Affaires.

I could not bear to see it die along with her. I was operating in my own traumatized state but did not want to further add to that trauma by severing the one thing we had shared. Not wanting French Affaires to die, would also mean learning how to make it live, now with me responsible.

> When you lose someone you love
> Your life becomes strange.

Having strangeness in acute form, due to the reality described here, I sought to find some kind of lifeline, some place that was not strange, that was at least the bearer of memories we had shared.

Everyone who has lost a loved one has some version of this painful strangeness. For many, if not all, it feels like death. And it is a kind of death. The strangeness of the space around me, without her in some memory form, and being traumatized, without the possibility of finding what was there vestigially to be found, I sought her in the France we had shared.

I would frequently say in these first months, I must find whatever available light there is and try to walk there. If light arises, cultivate it.

With this came a challenge. Running French Affaires is hard work, requires lots of planning and business skills, people skills, and promotional skills. The danger would be, that in going to where memories and the grief they engender live, the responsibilities of running the trips and making them work would be another set of tasks drowning out the woman who was my wife and whose memories I was seeking—for their own sake and because my life in the US was strange without her.

I was fortunate in finding—or being given—a companion, Maud Hacker, who would journey alongside me. French Affaires is a two-person job, minimally. Elizabeth had me (and various assistants). I did not have her. I am a man. French Affaires trips have lots of women. My new-found friend was a professional guide and a joy to be around. We have gone down many, many roads together.

This means, as well, that with a companion alongside, the space can open up to re-experience days and hours with Elizabeth, in the course of leading tours. The more I have done these trips—I thought I'd just face the ones that had been scheduled for 2021 and 2022, but it is now 2026 and twenty-five trips later—the more they allow me the scope to "see" my wife.

But I must be careful here. There is a sort of balance beam. Life goes on and it has its own challenges and rewards, but losing Elizabeth in the midst of that only pushes the work and love of grief away. You don't "get over" someone you have loved and lost. And to the degree that people encourage in you that idea, they are only driving this necessary work into hidden places where the irresolution will cry out for attention.

Grief is also not linear. It is the least linear thing in life, and so it thwarts quantitative schemes for its alleviation. Falling in love isn't linear, either. That's what makes it love. Love is a qualitative gift that reorders all foregoing "quality" and sets it in the shade of the loved one.

Because life moves on—Elizabeth died in 2021, it's now 2026—and because you move along inside of time, you may be tempted to think the loved one will dissipate in the manner of all fading memories. But the loved one is not a thing subject to the ravages of time. She came to me precisely out of the ravages of time to make me a different person.

And they shall become one flesh.

It was after several years of "life moving on" that I sensed I wasn't somehow facing the grief in its truest form. This, after ongoing talking therapy with professional guides who were indispensable. I believe I was trying to persuade myself that the passage of time was supposed to be doing the critical work just by virtue of its passing and moving along.

I was wrong about this.

In moving into more dedicated grief work, one thing I would realize is that the loss of a loved one scrambles the way time works. I knew that in glimpses, of course. But it is an overwhelming truth that cannot be gainsaid.

O'Donohue writes of the

> Days when you have your heart back,
> You are able to function well
> Until in the middle of work or encounter,
> Suddenly without warning
> You are ambushed by grief.

Grieving people know this, because its attacks are strong in the months following death. But in my view, versions of this live on, because grief has a unique character. Love is what is ambushing, because it has become a part of your deepest self and you miss it, and it wants to speak to you.

The spatial challenge of my own loss has made this more pronounced.

I will share just one story for now on this topic, this spatial challenge for me in my loss.

I was working on a trip with a colleague in the Var. I knew her from taking clients to the Isle of St. Honorat, lying off Cannes, where she organizes the wine tastings. I had always enjoyed seeing her.

She had phoned and wondered whether we might collaborate, an idea I had floated previously.

So, we were doing the kind of reconnaissance that is needed in order to organize a trip and offer it formally. Four days together. Lots of time to share stories and listen to the heart alive in them.

I had been doing trauma, or "complicated grief" work, with a professional outside of New York, thus via online sessions. I wanted to meet with her when I was in France, to stay on schedule. So, when our four days were finished, I had a (rare) free day to walk and process and get ready for our session.

It was by far the most intensely emotional session I'd had up to that point. I was not in any particular place in France that Elizabeth and I had shared. In fact, somewhat rarely, I was somewhere she and I had never been before.

A France more widely of our common life was rising up all the same. Perhaps speaking only French for four days, with a friend and companion, was helping, was bringing Elizabeth to me.

So, being in a new place didn't matter.

I had been walking a Stations of the Cross path above the village and had stumbled onto a Mass scheduled for just that "happenstance" timing.

It is here that I find Elizabeth most present to me. The French language of our shared life. The French Catholic phrasings of the liturgy that brought us together in worship. The general culture of the worshipers, the crying baby, the casual dress, the conduct, the kindnesses and awkwardnesses.

Elizabeth and I are together in worship, worried about her health condition, rejoicing in her recovery, silently side-by-side. Entering the one space, the one space of hope and of eternity, of the one who entered our time and space and defeated death.

Now a reality to be shared in a space of recognition.

The English poet John Betjeman begins the poem, "House of Rest," with this simple line: "Now all the world she knew is dead."

The poem is about a widow who has also lost all her sons in World War Two.

The final lines are these:

Now when the bells for Eucharist
   Sound in the Market Square,
With sunshine struggling through the mist
   And Sunday in the air,
The veil between her and her dead
   Dissolves and shows them clear
The consecration prayer is said
   And all of them are near.

3

The Sharing of *une Maladie Rare*

When Elizabeth was diagnosed with LAM disease, just two years into our marriage, we did not know what it was. Doctors might recall it from their medical school years but had never seen a case.

The one specialist who worked with Elizabeth was humble enough to say that his form of treatment was only to mitigate the effects, that is, removing enough lymph fluid so she could breathe: a tube surgically inserted in the bottom of the lung and brought around to her tummy, so that with vacuum bottles specially ordered, she could take the fluid off manually.

This and a special low-fat diet was all that could be done. She had to make do with this routine for two years, until we found a place for her at the National Institute for Health. I was on sabbatical in Lower Saxony and can recall the challenge of continuing this unusual regimen in Germany, including follow-ups with doctors knowledgeable about LAM.

The NIH removed the system and put her on a medicine they were experimenting with—ironically, a drug that was indicated for anti-rejection purposes.

I mention this only as general background. Elizabeth had an incurable condition that would never resolve itself, save through some breakthrough NIH experts might discover. If they were blunt enough to say it, she would have to decline slowly until it became necessary, in the end, to have a lung transplant. An intermediate procedure was ruled out due to the scarring the initial surgical tube system had brought about.

The reason I wanted to write about "a life lived well in France" was to indicate how, in spite of all this, Elizabeth and I carried on. The physical limitations, the drug regimen, and so forth did not prevent us from enjoying life, especially when we moved to France. The NIH had nothing more they could do. She would stay on the medicine they were experimenting with, and we would live our life in the enchanted countryside south of Paris. We had expert care in Paris, and in time a loving environment in which to begin the run-up work for those hoping to receive a life-saving lung transplant.

As I reflect on it now, I suppose the thing that most occupied our thoughts—her's quite directly, mine as her husband—was the knowledge that she had a condition that was incurable. We had done everything possible. The NIH knew they had reached the end of their care. No cure had been found and no new medicines were there to halt the decline. Elizabeth was a young and healthy fifty-one-year-old woman. Her body was, however, slowly diminishing, until before the transplant she was 30 percent under her body weight—an already slim figure becoming yet more so.

I have talked about the medical realties in Part Two above. I wanted in Part One to emphasize the rich life we maintained in spite of this slow decline into very diminished weight and respiratory machines keeping her alive.

It is hard to describe how this was affecting us, because the *maladie rare* was not an immediate killer but a slow-motion one, lasting six years. One thing that would never leave us was the fact that she would *never* get better . . . until one day she awoke from six days of forced coma, following a twelve-hour surgery, and was alive again. French lungs bringing her back to life. Diminishment giving way to recovery.

We did not get married at the advanced period of our life anticipating that it would be overlaid with an unknown and incurable disease. And I want to emphasize how much Elizabeth and I did not let that change our life and its joyous trails, alongside the hard ones. But it was a silent force to be reckoned with all the same. That she survived made all those hard trails disappear in a single vapor trail behind us.

It was hard for me to know what effect this was having on me, as I reflect on it now. When you are married and are not the one with the rare illness and the obvious physical decline—a decline she could hide from others but not from me—a form of love different from the love we so easily speak about allows you to move forward. I was no saint, and at times I sensed my exhaustion and frustration.

Elizabeth knew that too. That doesn't make it easier but harder. She is suffering and facing death. I am too, but in a different way. It is hard to get ahold of this because of the imbalance.

I want to share a story that touches on this theme.

I was in Normandy after her death from COVID, working on a trip.

I had some free time. I was in the charming seaside town of Honfleur and I wanted to visit Lisieux, an hour south in the Calvados Department, for Sunday service. Lisieux is the home of St. Therese, the Carmelite nun known in French as *la petite Thérèse* and in English as the Little Flower of Jesus. She died at twenty-four, having given her life in service of the poor.

It was a Sunday. I wanted to see the famous ancient Lisieux Cathedral. I parked and made my way there. It was a disappointment, and seemed a bit cast to the side. Surely this wasn't the place of tribute for the Little Flower of Jesus.

Questioning the woman at the reception, the answer was no. A modern basilica has been built to honor her. How far away? About a twenty-minute walk.

It was a bright spring day so I looked forward to stretching my legs. The basilica is on the highest point in Lisieux and so one can see it rising up before you as you approach. Stunning. I was in time for Sunday Mass, starting in fifteen minutes.

This gave me time to be seated and take in the glorious, colorful, uplifting interior. I won't try to describe it, not with Google to hand for the curious. I would later post photos at the French Affaires site.

One unusual thing about *la petite Thérèse* is how young she was and how almost immediately canonized. But a further distinctive thing is that she lived at the dawn of photography. So, there are large black-and-white photographic portrayals of her that ring the interior space along the ceiling line. From little girl, to novice, to nun serving the poor, and finally to her last days before she died.

We see her smiling in what would be her death bed. Praying there. Being cared for as death approaches. And then finally her no longer alive in this world. Her face peaceful. Like Elizabeth's when her last breath from French lungs left her body.

The service started and then I always feel at home. The beautiful French language and hymns. I sense my wife beside me as before.

When it came time to move forward to receive communion—the service had been majestic, the space luminous—I stood up to queue in the aisle.

I had noticed to my right a lovely young couple. Moving in my direction I made out that she was blind. He was helping her negotiate the narrow lane of the pew to the center aisle. I offered to help and she took my elbow for the short space to the aisle.

As they then took their place before me, side by side, him helping, I was given to see Elizabeth and me. Side by side. Elizabeth in a wheelchair, or with crutches, or just holding her own, as in earlier days. I'd often place my hands on her shoulder from behind as we made our way forward.

I believe God wanted me to see myself as he saw me. Alongside my wife with a *maladie rare* and me, her husband, with a role in that, which was costing me everything too.

I had struggled to understand what the life of love during the time of LAM meant on my side. Due to the imbalance.

I believe I will always struggle with that. But for a moment, in the basilica dedicated to the Little Flower of Jesus, I could see Elizabeth and me making our way up the receive the body of Christ.

As before, and forever.

4

Alive and on the Move—Quietly

As a Christian theologian and as a human being, I have never had any strong views on angels and their ministrations. Frankly, if I thought about it, I'd assume they want it that way.

Lots of surprises on our journey through LAM could fall into the terrain of "the angelic hosts" and their visitations. Dr. Marc Humbert saying, "We'll get you through this and run a marathon together." The team at the transplant hospital, especially the head surgeon, who preferred privacy to acclaim or even simple thanks. The housekeeper's young kids who'd send me emoticons of encouragement—the first ever to arrive on my sober cell phone. Père Mercier arriving at a time of deep discouragement, knocking on the gate to our house, and giving a look of recognition steeped in pastoral care over the decades. A congregation committed heart and soul to Elizabeth and me, strangers from a different land, washed up on the shore of their kindness. Elizabeth's roommate, from Vanderbilt, bathing and anointing Elizabeth before she died, so she could be my wife one last time before angels carried her home.

Being in France for four years now, after her passing, has given me occasion to sense their presence. I have spoken about the lack of "spatial recognition" in my present home in the US. One might suppose that angels ply their trade in overcoming time and space, in the name of eternity and heaven itself, where they abide.

That much I know. The specifics belong on their side of the transactions. I assume they want it that way.

I have wanted to help those grieving in the particularities of their own loss. I am sharing my own in the hope those grieving may locate themselves inside the territory of God's kindness toward them, "who every grief has known."

My older brother died suddenly at the age of seventy, two years ago. I speak frequently with my sister-in-law about her loss. We all have special challenges.

My brother was the rector of a church in the community where she still lives. He had recently retired but in the nature of their life together at the church, she continues to have friends who knew them both. One sees these friends and various aspects of the loved one arise. Grief shows its social face. My sister-in-law lost her husband in the context of those who knew him and miss him as well, and share with her the grief that is hers and theirs.

This belongs to the "spatial recognition" I referred to above.

At my birthday this year, in the community where I moved, where I am also the theologian at the local church, I have had to find a fellowship of friends. They did not know Elizabeth, and so I do not have the context of social grief my sister-in-law does.

This has made my grief experience different, and hard for reasons unique to my present life.

I have been reluctant to have people in my home, both because I have had to create a community after losing Elizabeth, and also because it is full of our things and represents something of her special presence with me given the lack of anything or anyone else. I have had to make a home—something that Elizabeth had done so well for us.

On my birthday, friends helped gather a small group for a celebration at my house.

Two in particular had earlier helped hang drapes and paintings when I was away on a trip to France. I returned to this finished work, tired from the familiar but long journey, and gasped in thanksgiving. They helped make a home for me. Next to the flowers on the countertop in my kitchen, a small note card read, "God did not forget you." I was moved in deep ways and sensed my exhaustion at having had to do so much. To deal with Elizabeth's things and to deal with her painful absence in my life in a strange place.

To find and make a home without her.

I had found a tape of Elizabeth's voice in archives at the French Affaires website. She was being interviewed about her decision to found this special business that she loved. It is amazing how much a voice carries a person. When Jesus speaks to Mary and says her name, after his resurrection, it triggers a deep recognition in her soul.

I had not listened to this audio recording as carefully before when she was alive. She talked about her love of things French and how that had arisen in her young life. She described her business and some adventures in France where mention of "my husband" placed me in the scene again. The interview was an hour long. I treasure it as connective tissue, especially given the challenge of lack of spatial and social links.

At the birthday celebration I decided to play another archived piece I found. This was a video podcast of Elizabeth in a lavender field below the lovely village of Les Baux-de-Provence. Here was where Elizabeth and I went on our first French date, a month after meeting in Dallas, around Palm Sunday 2009. We had returned here many, many times. I wrote a commentary on Colossians at the foot of Les Baux-de-Provence in a rented house in the middle of an olive grove. A favorite restaurant is in Mausanne-les-Alpilles, where we went to Palm Sunday service that year, and returned again and again. I have walked all the trails in the charming Alpilles region.

I take clients back here now in my years of running French Affaires. In the summer of 2024, I was in this same field with the woman sitting beside Elizabeth in the lavender field. The podcast was made in July 2021, just two months before her death.

I wanted to introduce Elizabeth to those who have become my neighbors. I wanted her at my birthday party, for me. I needed my church friends to know who I am as I know who I am: the husband of Elizabeth, with whom I shared a journey to victory, and one that ended painfully as it did, with her death from COVID.

Although I was on a hard journey with Elizabeth, that passed through victory and then on into death, I do not want to forget the angels, alive and on the move, silently. That have risen up around me, the husband of Elizabeth.

In France, Elizabeth and I, with Marcel, were able to travel and enjoy the many rich places on our doorstep. Burgundy is but two-and-a-half hours away and it was a frequent destination for date weekends. Beaune was a favorite place. On the way there from Paris one passes Vézelay.

The basilica in Vézelay is a magnificent eleventh-century edifice. Here Bernard of Clairvaux preached the second crusade. Richard the Lionheart passed by here en route to the third crusade. The church is dedicated to St. Mary Magdalene, and it sits at the top of the popular route to Santiago in Spain. Her penitence served as the model for penitent pilgrims.

Elizabeth and I visited it on a rainy, dreary day. The basilica was under renovation, so lots of scaffolding and spaces you could not visit. This in addition meant that the village was quiet, the bustling town put on hold until the return of tourists would rejuvenate the place. I recall wanting to get back to the car park. We were disappointed though we knew the work was essential.

I am now in Beaune (wine capital of Burgundy) fairly frequently with French Affaires guests. On a recent visit, we had a spare day when I would drive the clients up to Paris, while others would join me at the hotel at the airport, for early flights the following day.

We decided to stop to see Vézelay on our way and have a lunch in the mediaeval town of Noyers.

This time the weather was glorious. We were a small group, and so I parked the van and encouraged everyone to make their way up to the church. The path is relatively steep, as the basilica of Mary Magdalene sits high atop the village. The penitent climbed this street en route to the basilica and then on to the camino bound for Santiago.

One guest was a bit slower than the others and I said I would catch her up.

Parking in France involves a little drill. We have ours also in the US. There is a *horadateur*, a well-placed machine in the parking area where you head to pay to park your car. The drill requires you to know your license plate number. Rental cars will have plates with numbers that you don't have stored in your mind, so you take a picture and head to the *horadateur.*

It was Sunday and the lot was full. There was a queue at the pay station. This can often lead to frustration as people unaccustomed to the drill fumble around with the required keystrokes, license plate number entry, how-much-time buttons, and the contactless point where you hold your credit card. Some pay with cash, and that involves its own steep penitential climb.

You will know that at times like this a little recording starts playing in your head. Why can't they hurry up? Don't they know how the drill goes? Why are they trying to pay with cash? Tourists. And so forth.

I felt another distinct recording starting up in my head. Who cares? It is Sunday. A beautiful day. The trip is wrapping up. Everyone is just fine. Cool it.

The queue was down to one final couple. In their eighties I would guess. Handsomely dressed. Sunday best. She with a beautiful silk foulard, he in colorful slacks and sport coat. Married for a long season. Knew each other.

He was struggling with the machine. Maybe didn't have his glasses. Perhaps just the age where we didn't have to do this kind of thing before, darn it. His wife would call out the numbers of their license plate and he would fumble to enter.

Patient with each other. Kind.

No ticket coughed out. He tried a second time, a bit more diligently, eyes closer to the steel machine staring back at him. She trying to encourage him. Again, no success. Then a third time. Same result.

The language they were speaking was Italian and I don't know it for this kind of transaction. But they understood French.

I turned to them and said let's do this. Let me have a go. You watch over my shoulder. I think we can get this to work. I go through the (what are for me) familiar paces. Press this. Then that. Get iPhone photo of license number. Enter that, determine the time, hit pay, choose credit card option, hold card. Ticket printed and in its little trough for retrieval.

I turn and say, It works. Now, let's get your ticket. I coach him, if necessary, we walk through the steps, credit card at ready and out pops the wonted piece of paper, to be placed in the car behind the windscreen. They beam with joy. I throw a single Italian word at them and assume it wouldn't matter if accurate. Prego! We are speaking the language of patience and kindness. I say goodbye and we go to our cars with the pay tickets. I pass Madame again and smile. I climb to find my French Affaires guest happy at the many shops along the way.

As we approach the porch of this grand structure, I see it for the first time free of scaffolding. It is breathtaking. Sun setting it off brilliantly. The huge doors through which pilgrims have passed since the eleventh century. Moving.

We enter the building, and I remember it is Sunday. Mass is underway. The music soars. It is so beautiful, such a crowding of the senses, I gasp with tears of joy. My friend hands me a napkin from her purse as we sit for a moment to take it all in. The renovation has brought to full flower the beauty of the original structure. We listen to the chanting and hymns. The sermon begins.

Though a Sunday Mass, we are not the only ones present who have come simply to see the basilica itself. People are quietly moving along the side aisles, taking the beauty of the place in.

I move forward to glimpse the sanctuary area. I can recall standing here with Elizabeth when the building was under restoration, heaps of rubble and worship discontinued for a long season of dedicated labor.

I saw a beautiful sight. Seven nuns in white. In postures of prayer, immobile. Like ministering angels. I have been in a lot of abbeys, monasteries, basilicas, and cathedrals in France and I have never seen something like this. Immobile, silent, white figures bent in prayer and adoration.

Walking back, I would do what I always do. Light a votive candle for Elizabeth. My guest friend beside me.

I drop in the coins and pick up a candle from the rows on a tidy black stall. Lighted candles carrying prayers heavenward.

I search to find the long taper with which you catch a flame from another praying candle so as to light your own but cannot find it. This is not typical. Hmmm. Where is it? I try to light mine with another in its plastic encircled holder, but it won't do the trick.

At this point I turn to a rack just steps away to try and locate a taper there. And who is there? The lovely Italian couple.

They begin to search in earnest on my behalf. No, no taper here either. Worship is going on, so we silently shrug. I step to the rack with my candle to see if I have missed something.

The couple approach from my left. In their aging fingers they have brought me dried wax they have scraped up so as to help me, their eyes hopeful. I try fruitlessly to transfer fire to my candle with their wax, moved that they have sought to help me.

My friend hands me the napkin from her purse, which I had apparently returned to her, after drying my eyes. This will do the lighting.

I roll up the napkin and light it, then light my candle, carefully snuffing out the napkin. I place my lighted prayer candle in the midst of neighbors on the rack.

I am surrounded by a Holy Family. Heaven and earth are joined. I send my tears of love to Elizabeth, from the fire of Love that kindled it.

Angels prostrate in prayer.

5

French Language Life

LIFE GOES ON AFTER the loved one is gone.

I have been a writer all my life. As an academic, one writes books to get career advancement and a measure of professional security. I have been fortunate to have taught and trained many advanced, doctoral level students. To attract them, you write. They know you through your work.

Writing at this level is very hard work. Detailed work. Work in various research languages. Footnote factories. Lonely work.

You are also never able to gauge the impact you are making, in the widest sense. Sales figures tell you only so much, and they are deeply impersonal. You get glimpses when people reach out, or when students tell you they want to work with you because "you wrote that book and I want to learn more." Over time, you get used to the odd anonymity and isolation this career demands. You begin, if you are fortunate, to chase resolution on matters that have become important to you. Gaps, impasses, foreshortened perspectives, fresh horizons given the long journey you have been on, giving you the ability to look around intellectual corners.

I have also done a lot of preaching in my life. This is a different craft. You are writing to be heard. Punch, repetition, illustration, musical scoring. Movement between the hemispheres of the brain.

This writing can be done with a keen awareness of who you are talking to—rather like the occasional letters of Paul. But it isn't necessary. Paul wrote general epistles as well, and one can well imagine he was thinking of a wider audience and a greater afterlife when he moved into this genre.

The preponderance of my preaching has been like this.

I have also taught preaching and listened to a lot of very good preachers. Especially the latter have had a big impact on me. You begin to get a feel for the different rhetorical timing and tone. I covet the experiences of my life where I was able to hear transforming and deeply stirring preaching.

When I lost Elizabeth, I have been able to have recourse to my writing self. I have been able to do deeper spiritual direction and reflection, of the kind that pain and searching evoke. I have been able to tap into lectures and files that have stood ready for repurposing and a fresh hearing given the place I found myself after Elizabeth's death.

I do miss being able to share sermons and meditations with her. When we were first married, she helped me with public presentations, Lenten series, and other genre of writing. I was blessed to have married an intelligent, sharp, PhD-trained woman who happened to be beautiful, kind, and wise. We had each other's measure. In many ways, the idea that I would, equally, be able to continue French Affaires after her would likely not have surprised her. One brother of mine thinks she was giving me the business when she asked me to go to France before her unexpected decline and death.

That makes sense to me. I would never have imagined the French language competence I presently have. But the language train is one I ride on from station to station, and I have done likewise with several other languages. Learning languages teaches you how to handle confusion. You learn to accept 20 percent comprehension and see it as progress, until the number grows and becomes something like proficiency. In Part One, I reflect on the experience of learning a language and how it is a form of being born again, as a new language is born in you. Suddenly you find it is there, and that it precedes translating thought.

People would often ask me if Elizabeth was teaching me French. The obvious answer is, that is not the terrain for husband and wife.

I would now say, yes. But not as you meant it then.

When we were in France, I took every opportunity to learn French at immersion schools all over the country. I did Zoom French learning, there and here. Running French Affaires, French is a necessity, and she is the mother of invention.

I had been writing in more creative forms toward the end of my academic career. You get to do that. I was also living in France, so my sensibilities were changing. I taught a seminar at the Jesuit seminary in Paris on a figure whose work came alongside my own in intriguing ways, and he was unknown outside of French language settings. I wrote a book about that. It also required my translating portions of his work into English.

After I lost Elizabeth, I gave some lectures on Job and used them for a book which included personal anecdotes from my life. When you are doing advanced French language work, you are mostly just talking. The teacher keeps track of things to advise and correct.

So, what do you talk about? In my case, I told stories that came to mind and many of them were from my growing up years. So, I was tapping into this terrain already. It comes with age, as well.

I have just finished a writing project that involves research into the superintendent of finances under Louis XIV, a man whose name is Nicolas Fouquet. I had to read every recent biography of the man, and there is only one in English. Its subtitle is *The Man Who Outshone the Sun-King.*

I ask myself often how I came upon this project, and why was it speaking to me so deeply after Elizabeth's death.

Fouquet was the wealthiest and most influential man in France in the seventeenth century. He is known most for the chateau he built, Vaux-le-Vicomte. It was not far from our home in Courances.

Elizabeth got to know the owners. I have been there with her and then several times after her death. It is a very nice place to visit, and I prefer it to Versailles.

Fouquet was charged with treason and embezzlement. He was tried and sentenced with lifetime imprisonment. Voltaire would say about him, "On August 21 at 6 p.m. he was the king of France and at 2 a.m. he was a nobody."

He was exiled to the Savoie, to the royal prison of Pignerol. His valet was the enigmatic figure known by posterity as the Man in the Iron Mask. He died there after sixteen years, just before his release, at age sixty-five.

I think it must have been the crashing loss of everything dear to him that brought his life close to mine, in this present period. I was also comparing him to the voice that appears in the book of Ecclesiastes, where a king has crashed and burned and is giving penitent counsel shortly before his death.

Tragic loss, death, the French language searching for a man and his life that went away.

Just in the way these things happen, I had been sent an online link to a sermon I gave on Ecclesiastes. A friend had seen it and sent it to me, in the days after the loss of my wife. The title was "The Preacher Says

Goodbye." Elizabeth was alive and in the congregation when I gave this address. She was seated right up front where I could see her.

The colleague who had invited me was in the congregation and he knew Elizabeth's survival story. He and his wife had visited us shortly afterward in France. I mentioned as an aside from the pulpit that unlike the dying preacher in Ecclesiastes, my wife's life had been spared. It was a moment of thanksgiving and relief and I sensed it as I spoke.

I watched it now, for the first time, in some kind of oddly suspended time warp. I am speaking to her about her survival, with joy and relief. And yet, when it was sent to me to listen to, she was gone.

> When you lose someone you love.
> Your life becomes strange.

To deal with that loss, I write. I followed the trail of the language we shared, to the place we shared, to a man who lost everything, and who also, before his death, recovered his spiritual bearings. In prison he became a free man. Solomon contrite, the Ecclesiast, had become his companion and guide.

When Jesus called out to Mary in Aramaic and she responded "Rabbouni" it was in their shared tongue. "Teacher!" she gasped in joy.

In the time I had with Elizabeth on her death bed, after life-support was withdrawn, I spoke to her in the language we shared, as I had spoken to her in a hospital bed in the suburbs of Paris. French was our language, the language of our journeys. The language she adored as a young girl and that she mastered as a grown woman.

Yes, I learned French from my wife.

At her resting place here in the land of her birth, the grave marker reads,

> La roi d'amour est mon berger.
> Elizabeth New Seitz.
> Ma femme. Belle. Forte. Fidèle.
>
> The King of Love Is My Shepherd.
> Elizabeth New Seitz.
> My wife. Beautiful. Strong. Faithful.

I have had to carry on beyond this time. As every grieving person must. Writing has helped process the life in France we shared, and continue to share.

What of our shared language, shared life, shared journey?

A story again, from after this hard moment, Elizabeth's final time with me on earth.

It will be a story of worship again.

I have struggled to "see" Elizabeth in my mind's eye. Photos capture a moment in time, and they convey her to me. But the effect is two-dimensional.

I was with a group, again in Beaune, and a decision was made to find a church service on Saturday evening. Exceptionally, for the first Saturday–Sunday of the month, the location posted was a street address in the suburbs north of town. About twenty minutes on foot.

As we made our way there, I asked myself, since we passed an ancient parish church on our walk, what could this location be? Maybe the rectory? A small group of dedicated worshipers gathered around the priest, perhaps?

As we made the last turn and approached the Google-map destination, I saw a sign: A Senior Living Facility. And, being in France, a happy and well-maintained place. Just like all the French healthcare places Elizabeth and I knew so well.

Paintings by the senior citizens were posted on the walls as we made our way down the corridor, to a large public space. It had been turned into a chapel for the service. An altar table, and two people on guitar and vocals and (as we would learn) saxophone. I spoke to the priest and explained we were visitors. He was happy to receive us. A room full of people in various states of mobility, perhaps fifty or so, ranged in rows set up for the Mass.

A friend in our group turned to me and said, I'd like to be here too.

There was something tremendously optimistic about the place and the feel. Ladies in pretty outfits, their hair done for the occasion. Men in walkers or seated who had been well cared for and well groomed. The priest giving out a spirit of strength and hope and regularity—we were not in a place of dying but of living.

A more beginner-level French student was on my right, a woman herself in her sixties. I was trying to help our small group with the service book and the basics for negotiating the service (hymns, refrains, when to stand and sit, how to receive communion).

A lovely elderly woman arrived late and sat down next to the beginner-level student to my right, all smiles. All nicely dressed up and ready for the most important event in her life. As life was now moving toward eternal life.

Out of the corner of my eye, I saw this woman asking for help with the numbers for hymns and place in the service book, leaning into our beginner to her left. The two got to know each in the way confusion and the patterns of worship ask. Smiling, yes, try this. I would feed her bits of information as best I could. The charming elderly woman was all good will and enthusiasm.

At a moment during the offertory, guitar player moved to saxophone. It was sheer beauty, imitating the happiness we all felt in this space. God playing his saxophone from heaven, looking down with joy and divine saxophone happiness.

I know the service by heart and the responses come back to me.

When we come to the line, after consecration of the elements, before communion, *je ne suis pas digne de te recevoir, mais dis seulement la parole et je serai gueri*, I can see—not in photo nor in two-dimension—my Elizabeth face-to-face.

Words that had carried us along through a trial, among friends, with clergy who loved us and were our stalwart Christian companions. Words that bring Elizabeth to me and assure me, in my spatial void and social void, God knows what he is doing now in my life. Even though I don't.

"Speak the word only and my soul shall be healed."

In English, in French, in Italian kindness and concern, for advanced and beginner, young and old, a Pentecostal life-giving Word of transformation and Life Eternal.

Ma femme. Belle. Forte, Fidèle.

> Gradually, you will learn acquaintance
> With the invisible form of your departed;
> And when the work of grief is done
> The wound of loss will heal
> And you will have learned
> To wean your eyes
> From that gap in the air
> And be able to enter the hearth
> In your soul where your loved one
> Has awaited your return
> All the time.

6

The Unspent Love

After you lose your loved one, grief is the love you cannot give.
The unspent love.

In what I am writing I am expressing the love I cannot give to Elizabeth. The unspent love. Now that she is gone from me. It is there because there was a lot of it, that we gave and returned, and I cannot give it now.

There is also the love I *could* not give. I want to try to write about that. It is a bit more difficult.

O'Donohue writes,

Your heart has grown heavy with loss
And though this loss has wounded others too
No one knows what has been taken from you
When the silence of absence slips in
Flickers of guilt kindle regret
For all that was left unsaid or undone.

"Flickers of guilt kindle regret." Where does this guilt come from? One must track it down. This, too, is a form of love. Belongs to love. The love that senses more could have been given, more love expressed, more patience shown. More time to ask as tenderly as possible, how is it going?

Why, when you lose someone you love, do these thoughts arise, these flickers of guilt? Sometimes stronger than flickers, depending on who you are and who you have lost.

I believe all of this is measured by the depth of love that has been given and expressed. The greater that depth, the more one knows that a purity of love demands all of us.

And yet, because love is borrowed from God, we are not its source and cannot give it as he does, who is Love itself.

I spoke of the love *I could not give*. Why was that? What happened?

When I go down the trail of love to answer that question, I can find thoughts arising. Times when I was at my wits end. Times when I was afraid. Times when being the one who was not ill and who had to be strong, or at least present with all I *could* give, simply took too much out of me.

And when love lies at the center, the loved one, the cared-for one, knows that too. Flickers of guilt likely arise on their side. I cannot know that, of course. In the context of pain and survival, language takes a different form. Our world of daily language is asked to go somewhere else, even beyond its capacity.

This is what disease and hardship and the approach of death bring upon us. In the rush of what is happening, Elizabeth, can you hear me? Can I be heard by you? I speak here more of the COVID season than her life saved in France. We could process things there. LAM was a companion for a long time. I was able to be with her before the lungs arrived, as together we waited, during brief visits allowed at the hospital.

When Elizabeth's life was saved in Paris, I recall that it took several days before she could let herself smile and comprehend what she had gone through. That she was truly alive. Six years is a long time to go downhill. Six days in a coma produced by strong medicines is a world one struggles, alive to be sure, to come out of. A new and strange world entered, even as it is a world of life with death now behind.

Or, because of that. That miraculous recovery. How am I alive? How did I come through all that?

Looking at calendar diaries now, I see a month's worth of intensive follow-up, up to Paris, IV transfusions given in our home, the gradual reduction of the first round of strong anti-rejection medicines. That meant she could be on her own, alive again. Learning to use her French lungs. For the very first time. Like a young infant learning to walk again.

But it was also hard work for her. She bought a lovely French pill dispenser, little cradles to hold daily doses, marked *lundi, mardi, mercredi, jeudi, vendredi, samedi, dimanche*, the days of the week, in a kid leather purse.

On Mondays, each week, she would carry in her big Carrefour shopping bag full of medicines. Collected from the local pharmacy. She would find a comfortable spot and begin organizing the daily doses to be put in this dispenser kit. It became unto her proximate and necessary, a bit like the respiration equipment. Now breathing into her what she needed, what her French lungs transplanted into her chest, needed. So she could live.

I wrote "A Breath of French Air" about a year after Elizabeth's transplant.

It was a special story to write because I knew the outcome. She had made it. I had made it. We had our life back.

Yet Elizabeth, while alive, had a demanding discipline to continue. The medicines could be hard on her. The teams that worked with her post-transplant sought to help regulate dosages, to prevent migraines and nausea. They didn't always get it right.

Here is where our gratitude for being alive diverged. Elizabeth still had the medical regimens to follow.

Also, how long could one live after a lung transplant? The statistics say that for most people it is five to six years, but a decade and longer are not to be ruled out. For the healthy, and those with a double lung transplant, the odds improve.

Elizabeth had to carry this reality around with her. In looking back at a calendar entry, I see all the continued movement of our life in 2019. Yet, uncharacteristically, I see a note in her hand in an empty date box, which reads, "Little did I know I was about to live a medical marathon of the worst kind." How I ache when I read that. A window into what post-transplant could at times feel like to her.

As for the longevity topic itself, we didn't talk about it. We knew the statistics cited above and Elizabeth knew she was healthy and strong. The doctors reviewed the charts with us. I assumed, given her health and her discipline, that she would be among those for whom the odds for longer life were good. The migraines and nausea were intrusions, not steady state.

But most of all, for me, it was the fact that she had survived that dominated. That we were able to continue our life together. To travel, to enjoy each other's company, to be husband and wife without the respiratory machines and the LAM journey of decline.

The reason Elizabeth did not write the chapters of "A Breath of French Air" alongside mine has its likely answer here. The exhilaration and victory I wanted to convey would not be shared by her in such a way that our paths overlapped in telling a story.

In searching for a way to communicate the unspent love after her death, I have come upon this hard truth.

This also means that when COVID arrived, it was hard for me to gauge its potential for threatening Elizabeth's life. We'd had two-and-a-half years post-transplant in France. Our life had moved on.

And no one really knew what kind of reality COVID represented. I don't think we know that now.

On my side of the ledger, we had fought LAM and won. It had taken a lot out of me, physically, emotionally, spiritually. I wanted that struggle to be over. I wanted to be able to live my life again, with a healthy Elizabeth. It looked like, from every side, that was possible now. The decline to death was over. The exertion related to that was over.

To think otherwise was to have run a marathon and as the tape appeared ahead, to have it removed, and set up at a distance I could not see.

And this is what happened. For us both. Not initially—the disease left us alone. In 2020 I returned to seminar teaching—now online—and Elizabeth taught French and held webinars. We travelled domestically. Church was outside, so we could attend and be careful. Then home communion to be safe.

As I reflect on it now, even 2020 had a sad aura about it. I missed France, and moving to a new place is always a challenge. I hadn't planned to go back to work. We had bought a big house and Elizabeth lost her income and livelihood when COVID killed international travel. I am quite sure that in some part of me the new marathon tape I couldn't see just wearied and exhausted me. We had been through so much already. It hurt that Elizabeth would have to struggle with post-transplant life. As I said, it was an intermittent thing, but I wanted a full return to health. I wanted the wife I married back again. How could this be happening?

During this time, in 2021, we also had work going on at our house. We were closing in two sleeping porches and it was a big job. Invasive at times. Noisy.

It began to look like the skies were clearing in the summer of 2021. We had avoided COVID. Got the vaccines, Elizabeth in consultation with her medical team in Charleston.

In July we flew to France. Such a great thing to be able to return after so much isolation. I rented a car and we drove down through Burgundy, spent a night, and then on to Provence. The owner of a new *relais chateau* high-end lodging, north of Aix-en-Provence, had gifted Elizabeth (aka

French Affaires) three free nights, in the hopes of attracting business. COVID was no friend to the travel industry.

Oh, what a lovely time it was. I have that precious video of Elizabeth happy in the lavender field that I will treasure all my life.

We then drove to our former home village and spent four nights with friends. Walked old paths. Then up to Paris. I can see the big lumbering aircraft doing drills over the Paris sky in the run-up to 14 July, la Fête Nationale.

It would be our last time together in France.

Upon return, I contracted COVID. I stayed in the garage apartment, in isolation. Probably got it from the workers in the house. Elizabeth would place trays of food at the foot of the stairs.

I thought to myself. I am being cared for by my wife. The tables are turned. She is good at this. I am exhausted.

Then she got COVID. I suspect from the same source as me.

This is when I fought to keep my sanity. No. No. Not again. With the disease still giving me aches some days after it passed, I drove Elizabeth to Charleston Medical University Hospital. The same length drive as up to Paris. No. No. Not again.

How could this possibly happen to us again? Fear and commitment to hard work to do what is necessary, in equal measure.

Here is where I wish I could have found more love. I just felt like I was hitting a wall. I could not accept that Elizabeth, and I, were going into medical hell one more time.

There is not much to say. Those who know this reality will understand.

I believed she would not be defeated. She could not be robbed of life after what she had endured. Indeed, she did stabilize. After two weeks. And we could communicate during this time, when she was able.

What to do with all the trips lined up? I don't want to get trapped in details here, as my intention is different. I just could not see French Affaires die as I knew how much it meant to her. One trip was cancelled. We would hold on.

I was able to visit Elizabeth at last. Through a plate glass window. Then the doctors allowed me to visit, two days later. Their view was it was time to organize out-patient dialysis. Elizabeth had stabilized. As for French Affaires, they said it was occupying her too much, and that she needed to rest. If I took the trip for her, that would help.

With all that as backdrop, I left the following day and promised to stay in touch. It was a seven-day trip and I'd be back soon.

In my mind, I was fighting for my wife again. Fighting for a life we had shared. Fighting for a life I believed we would be sharing after she came out of the hospital. I'd bring Marcel to the dialysis center so he could see her.

Instead, she went downhill three days after I was in France. Her close friend—a nurse—graciously spent about two days with her. I would need to come back as soon as I could.

I handed the trip on to helpers I arranged. I said goodbye to our chauffeur and close friend and made the trip back. Lyon, Paris, JFK, Savannah. I have made that trip in years since and don't know how I managed. I spent the night in our home and drove up the next morning. She was in bad shape and unable to speak with me.

I have been trying to express the feelings of utter confusion, exhaustion, not-again, unfair, she'll put on her war paint and win all the same. That was not to be the ending. When asked if she would be willing to go on life-support, I had no idea just what that meant in the specifics of her situation.

When Carol phoned me in France, she asked Elizabeth if she wanted me to come home. And she asked Elizabeth to say it aloud in her own voice. She did. "Chris, I want you to come home."

That was the last time I would hear her voice.

When asked about intubation, only days later, I was next to her. She looked at me and shook her head. No. A pause, and she nodded. Yes. She reached up and held my cheek with her left hand. Even then, I assumed she would fight and win. I had nothing to go on but the years together with a woman whose strength was one of the things that made our love what it was. My strong and beautiful Elizabeth.

Someone wrote, and I started with this:

> Grief, I've learned, is really just love. It's all the love you want to give but cannot. All that unspent love gathers itself inside your heart, eyes, some hollow and aching part of your chest. Grief is love with no place to go.

I am trying to give expression to the love God allowed Elizabeth and me to share. A love that traversed mountains and valleys. A love shaped in the crucible of illness and victory. A love that was expressed, given and received, and the love that was hard to express in times of sheer agony.

The agony of having to go a second time into a place of suffering and, this time, death.

The flickers of regret hover over all that we endured together, and are a part of the love we shared, when we were asked to bear so very much.

I have written this Part Three because there is a hearth in the soul. The hollow and aching part of your chest is not all that is to be said. But it is a part. I needed to speak of that as belonging to the journey of love.

I have a loved one whose loss is unbearable at times. But at other times she enters my soul and I know I have had a love like nothing else as true in my life.

Elizabeth. My wife, beautiful, strong, faithful, forever. I love you.

CONCLUSION

In the providence of God, the last time I heard Elizabeth's voice was in France. I was there continuing her beloved French Affaires. In her place. I would wrap that trip up and return to see her alive, having again fought off a deadly disease.

Also in the providence of God, that did not happen. God took Elizabeth home.

I do not know if she would have imagined my continuing her work in France for more than four years now. I have indicated the reasons why I have struggled to hear her voice here in the place we tried to make a home.

The drama of a COVID arrival and death made our return here a vague and watery place, especially now with her gone. It is natural, I suppose, that the place where she outdistanced LAM and where we had "A Life Lived Well in France" has continued to speak to me, and to bring her to me in ways I find almost impossible here.

There, I hear her voice again.

This last installment, "The Love That Grief Is," is my best effort to find the love that rises up after she is gone. In seven brief sections. The final one is necessary to bring the story to its conclusion. It is also the hardest of the seven to tell. We had to go one more time into the breach. Just writing it up exhausts me because it is a story of exhaustion after victory, and a cruel robbery of that.

The love that Elizabeth and I shared meant we both had to experience that. Each in our own way, and as a couple.

French Affaires and our life in France were not anything I would have imagined when I married Elizabeth. I'd had a lot of adventures and a life of living abroad. Ironically, LAM disease forced our hand a bit and pushed us France-ward in ways we had not planned, and which enriched us enormously. It was also the place where we faced death—Elizabeth first-hand, me as her husband—and it did not win. She won. We won.

I also believe living in France made that happen. Not only the expert healthcare and transplant team, but also the enlivening effect France had on Elizabeth. She was living the dream of her life. That is surely a spectacular medicine.

I do not know where my life leads now.

I do know about a hearth where Elizabeth lives now. I want that space to grow. Until I see her at the eternal hearth.

And I am glad that the story I tell here, to conclude this book, is 6/7ths blessing. I want that balance sheet to reflect God's perfect intentions for me and for those he loves in his Son.

Even as now I walk alone and seek to find the light he shines in dark places.

I have told a story that has no conclusion. I read these lines recently in a post of Rod Dreher and they speak to me: "Nothing we make here will be eternal, but we have to build them as if they will be eternal. . . . That's what God wants. If you promise yourself to a woman for a lifetime, that is a way of making the eternal present here in time."

Eternity is the conclusion. A living on forever in the overflowing bounty of God's time.

And for me in the story of *Le Grand Voyage* I offer here.

www.ingramcontent.com/pod-product-compliance
Lightning Source LLC
LaVergne TN
LVHW091124080826
845145LV00008B/2038

* 9 7 8 1 6 6 6 7 1 1 5 9 2 *